Elaine Slater's
BOOK OF NEEDLEPOINT PROJECTS

Elaine Slater's

BOOK OF
Needlepoint
Projects

ILLUSTRATIONS BY LISA LEVITT

HOLT, RINEHART AND WINSTON

NEW YORK

Copyright © 1978 by Elaine Slater

All rights reserved, including the right to reproduce this book or portions thereof in any form.

Published simultaneously in Canada by Holt, Rinehart and Winston of Canada, Limited.

Library of Congress Cataloging in Publication Data

Slater, Elaine.
Elaine Slater's book of needlepoint projects.

1. Canvas embroidery. I. Title. II. Title:
Book of needlepoint projects.
TT778.C3S57   746.4'4   78-2597
ISBN 0-03-017516-X

FIRST EDITION

Designed by Betty Binns
Illustrations by Lisa Levitt
Photographs by Jim Chambers

PRINTED IN THE UNITED STATES OF AMERICA

10   9   8   7   6   5   4   3   2   1

To my four generations:

Pauline and Abe who were always there.
Mae who always took pride.
Jimmy always always.
And to my four children who have become thirteen:

Michael and Kathy
Ken and Brenda
Lisa and Will
Abigail
and . . .

Nathaniel
Joanna
Simon
Aaron
Eli
Alexander

Contents

Working from Graphs

Eight pages of color photographs follow page 142.

Acknowledgments

Writing a book not only calls on the author's resources, but on the talent, support, and enthusiasm of many others. I am indebted to friends, customers (many of whom I look upon as good friends), and to all of those who have offered suggestions and help.

I am grateful to Judi Alweil of Gemini for letting me use the Harper's Lady to demonstrate stitches.
To Bonnie Nathanson of Sunshine Designs for allowing me to use the Greenhouse canvas.
To Kathi Woodard of K-W Designs for permitting me to feature the On the Town Canvas.
To Aaron Russo of Artists Entertainment Complex and Divine Pictures as well as to Atlantic Recording Co. for letting me re-create Bette Midler's striking face on needlepoint.

To C. Richard Brose of Schumacher who gave me the go-ahead on using the Schumacher fabric for my pillow.
And there are a special few for whom appreciation should be given with an abundance of thanks and affection.

To Per Buan, a friend and gentleman whose help in so many ways, given unsparingly, made a difficult task much easier. His artistic and technical skill produced the Indian Rug, and, utilizing the techniques taught in my advanced class in needlepoint, he worked the beautiful Geometric Sampler.

To Mrs. Margaret Little, for her patience and generosity in allowing me to borrow her lovely Floral Rug and her beautiful Wallpaper-Motif Vest for many months during the preparation of this book. These were among the first things that Mrs. Little ever attempted in needlepoint, and are, I believe, a great tribute to her skill and artistry.

And how do I thank Abby Slater, who volunteered to proofread the entire manuscript, checking all measurements and pointing out and correcting errors. Her help was very meaningful to me and lightened the load considerably, while her buoyant spirit and absolute dependability were a great comfort to me.

As was the help of Lisa Spotnitz, a New Yorker, who ran innumerable errands for me in connection with the preparation of this book, and who found time to work the Bette Midler record cover in needlepoint while simultaneously caring for her young baby and doing graduate studies.

And I must also thank two other associates on whom I have relied so heavily: Lisa Levitt, my illustrator, whose skill, hard work, and good nature I could always depend on; and Jim Chambers of the Art Gallery of Ontario, my photographer, for his willingness always to try for "one more shot," for his prompt responses to my calls for help, and for the technical excellence he brings to his work.

Introduction

For many years needlepoint was considered something for "little old ladies." This was largely because of the so-called Berlin canvases that were stamped out by the thousands in the early part of this century. They always had the same sentimental scene, always the same purse with cabbage roses on a black, wine, or beige background, always the same chair seat with a wreath of flowers. Often the centers were pre-worked, so the ladies had nothing to do but toil away at the endless boring background, robbed of all the fun and creativity.

It was different hundreds of years ago, when needlepoint first came into its own. Then it was an art form. It was different from other forms of needlework in that it was not primarily useful or practical, but rather a decorative thing of beauty. During the Middle Ages, needlepoint was used to bring color and beauty to rough stone walls, and only incidentally to keep out the drafts that swept through chinks in the stones. Mary, Queen of Scots, spent her last hours needlepointing adornment for her tester bed. Perhaps Shakespeare's Hamlet ran his sword through needlepoint when he stabbed Polonius cowering behind the "arras" covering the wall.

Needlepoint was born as an art form, and that is what I would like to return to it—and to you, the reader.

My first book, *The New York Times Book of Needlepoint*, taught needlepoint through the use of a single project, a sampler. I taught about ten different stitches, using graph after graph to guide the learner each step of the way. Because I received so many grateful letters from people who in this manner were able to learn stitches that had previously been baffling, I have decided to use the same method to teach another group of exciting stitches. In addition, instead of concentrating on a single project, this book offers a wide range of projects that utilize various techniques.

It is my firm belief that the seed of genuine creativity exists in all of us if we can only release it. Some of us—most often from a lack of self-confidence—need more help in getting that seed to flower. Others need only a touch of support—an idea, a suggestion—and growth begins at once. This book is designed for both groups. It will provide fertile ground for those who require very little help, and it will give support and direction to those who need a bit more in order to get that seed to sprout. But watch out. Once it starts to grow, there is no stopping it!

Creativity in needlepoint can take many different directions: working with painted canvases; graphing designs; tracing other patterns, etc. I have tried to reach out to as many people as possible by presenting a potpourri of projects that encompass a wide range of these various approaches. These projects will all be found in Part Two of the book.

There are those who would like to learn how to "paint" with yarn. Here the needlepointer starts out with an entirely blank canvas, working a design based solely on the yarn color and various types of stitches. Projects using this technique include the Rainbow Wall-hanging, the Irish Village Pillow, the Firecracker Bolster, and the small Geometric Sampler.

Others would like to be able to reproduce—with a minimum of effort and expense—designs that they have discovered in magazines or on wallpaper, fabric, record cover albums, etc. It is quite amazing what we see around us once our eyes are opened to the possibilities. Then we discover designs everywhere, from a cocktail napkin to a cereal box or toothpaste tube. The projects in this book that involve tracing designs include such diverse items as a grandchild's drawing, a swatch of fabric, a record cover, a portrait, a wallpaper pattern from which a vest was fashioned, my own designs for small director's chairs for children, and a doorstop.

And then there is always the painted canvas that you fall in love with. Although it was not painted or designed by you, it nonetheless expresses your personality in some indefinable way. What fun it is to take such a canvas and transform and individualize it through the use of imaginative stitchery until it becomes your own unique creation. I have selected three painted canvases that appealed to me. If they appeal to you as well, you can find out where to purchase them in the "Shopping Guide" on pages 189–90. But even if your taste runs to something quite different, this book will nonetheless tell you how to add interest and personality to any painted canvas.

There are some people who love the precision and clarity of graphs. They do not wish to work in any other way. These people want to know that what they see is what they are going to get. They have the option of making changes, but that is their choice. They also have the option of precise replication, if that is what they want. For these people, I have graphed some very beautiful designs that include a Floral Rug, an Indian Rug, a Skirt Border, a Decorative Panel, and an Alphabet Pillow.

It is a great convenience to have a graphed alphabet, so I have included a very playful one on pages 172–84. Use it to form initials, words, even sayings. You can make it larger or smaller by simply changing the mesh size.

Most readers will want to begin by working a favorite project. I hope that after this is completed, you will attempt one or both of the samplers described in the section "Working on Blank Canvas" (pages 140–50), so you can utilize more of the lovely stitches described in Part One. From that point on, you should feel confident enough to try your hand at all the different methods described herein to create a work of art.

Which method do I prefer? All of them, at one time or another. I have worked projects using every technique described here. I love precision and order. I love flexibility and discovery. I love transforming an existing work of art.

But once again, in this book I shall try not to let you down. I shall follow you through every possible difficulty, warning you in the stitch texts of errors to be avoided, and giving you multiple diagrams of every stitch, plus additional diagrams illustrating stitch variations.

And because I know how frustrating it is to be eager to start a project only to find that you have no idea of the amount of yarn needed, I shall tell you exactly how much yarn to purchase for each project. Although in most cases I will specify color, I hope that you will go off on your own sometimes and select the colors that most suit you.

I have included a chapter at the end of the book, "Blocking and Finishing," which tells how to put your needlepoint into its final form. I have consulted with experts and will give you a brief idea of what can be done to complete each project. But I do recommend that if you are like me—not an experienced seamstress or framer—it is best to have your work finished by an expert. This will give it the professional appearance that so many loving hours of care and work deserve.

Now, thumb through the book, find a project you would like to get started on, and begin. Remember that the fun is in the doing, not in the completion, so don't rush things. Enjoy the creative aspect. You will find that you do some of your best thinking when you are not working at your piece, but when your mind is nonetheless mulling over all the stitch, color, and design possibilities.

Needlepoint is fun. Needlepoint is a challenge. It is a relaxing pastime, and the final result is a thing of beauty!

Elaine Slater's
BOOK OF NEEDLEPOINT PROJECTS

Questions and Answers
About Needlepoint

It is important to read the entire "Questions and Answers" section before beginning your first project. It will help you to get started, may answer questions that have puzzled you in the past, and I hope it will solve any problems before they arise.

NEEDLES AND YARN

How do you select the proper type of needle for various meshes?

Tapestry needles have blunt rather than pointed ends. The needle number goes higher as the mesh count per inch goes higher. Therefore, while a 10 or 12 mesh will use a #18 needle, 14 or 16 mesh will use a #20 needle, and 18 mesh or higher will use a #22 needle.

Is the same type of needle used for quickpoint?

Yes. A 5 or 7 quickpoint canvas uses a #13 tapestry needle. This is sometimes hard to find, but a "knitter's needle," which is a rather blunt-pointed needle used to sew knitted sections together, will do.

Are all yarns suitable for needlepoint?

No. There is a wide variety of yarns—such as Persian wool, linen, cotton and silk embroidery floss, and metallics—that are appropriate for needlepoint and that add interest and texture. A type that should *not* be used, however, is knitting yarn; this stretchy, short-fibered yarn will fray quickly. If you think about it, you will realize that knitting yarn only touches your knitting needles twice—once as it is wound around the needle and once as it is knitted off the needle. But a strand of needlepoint yarn gets pulled through the canvas again and again—as many as seventy times or more, depending on the length of the strand.

If a single strand of needlepoint yarn must take so much wear, what is the best length strand to use?

To avoid fraying, I recommend that your strand be no more than 24 inches long when using 2- or 3-ply Persian yarn, for Basketweave, Continental, or intricate decorative stitches, and even shorter when using 1-ply. For Bargello work (which is basically the Brick stitch) and for other large, simple decorative stitches, 36-inch strands may be used.

Many shops sell yarn only by the yard. Should I order it uncut?

Because I am aware that most shops sell yarn either by the yard or by weight measure, I have given all yarn estimates in this book in yards and ounces. To translate this back to 24-inch strands, you need only add back half the yard estimate. For example, if a project calls for 30 yards of one color yarn, add half (or 15 strands) to that, and purchase or cut from uncut lengths 45 strands, each 24 inches long.

Which yarns are suitable for needlepoint, and where can I get them?

The "Shopping Guide" at the back of this book will tell you where you can write to find out who in your area might carry the following yarns.

Wool. There are many varieties of wool tapestry yarn. I prefer Persian yarn, which is a 3-ply yarn. The strands are twisted together in such a way that they can be easily separated. These yarns are produced by quite a few companies today, but the softest and loveliest, with the widest and most subtle color range, are those made by Paternayan Bros. in New York City and by Colbert in France. Paternayan "Paterna" yarns come in over three hundred shades, Colbert in almost two hundred. They are extremely versatile as they can be used as 3-ply yarn on a 10 mesh canvas, 2-ply on 12 mesh, and 1-ply on smaller mesh.

Cotton. These are made by many companies—notably DMC and Anchor—primarily for embroidery. But they are perfectly suitable for needlepoint, and add a pleasant sheen where highlighting is desired. The "pearl" type gives a special look that adds interest to canvases requiring a very high shine in certain areas. Cotton is also useful to people allergic to wool.

Linen. This type of thread has been hard to come by in the past. It generally originates in England or Sweden. Linen imparts to your work a dull homespun look that is most attractive. It is very effective in pulled-stitchery work.

Silk. This thread, usually made up of six or more very fine strands, is quite expensive and quite beautiful. It gives a richer and more subtle gloss to your work than cotton floss, but it is more difficult to use because it tends to tangle easily. Due to its fragile nature, it is best worked in short strands of 8–10 inches. Rubbing a strand on wax (an ordinary candle will do) helps prevent tangling and fraying.

Velvet. This is a specialty yarn that has velvet finish. It works best on a 12 mesh and is most effective where either a velvety texture or a clean line without the "fur" of wool is desired. It frays fairly easily, so it should be used in short lengths. Geometric or Bargello designs are very well suited to this yarn.

Metallic. This type of yarn comes in several colors in addition to gold and silver. It is extremely effective where appropriate, and should not tarnish. It can be difficult to work with, as the ends tend to split. I have found it helpful to break—not cut—it into 10-inch strands and then dip the ends of each strand into a drop of liquid glue—such as Sobo—or into clear nail polish. Allow the strands to dry; and you should not have any more trouble with split ends.

Synthetics. These yarns look and feel much like wool. They are a good substitute where allergies are a problem. They do not, however, wear quite as well as wool and tend to fuzz on the surface. They are less expensive than wool.

Rug Yarn. This is a heavier yarn that is very suitable for 5-mesh rug canvas. It is widely available in synthetics in a rather limited but basic color range. Paternayan Bros. produces a pure wool type, however, with a very wide color range. Note that all rug yarns specified are for Paternayan. Synthetics are much lighter in weight.

Is yarn usually purchased by length or by weight?

Both. Persian yarn is usually available by weight, but when it is sold in cut lengths, each length is usually a yard long. Some shops, such as my own, sell it in 24-inch lengths. As other yarns may be sold only by weight, I will give both yard and ounce estimates for every project.

Are your estimates down to the last strand?

No. I have always allowed plenty of room for errors that might involve a certain amount of ripping! Moreover, where length measures are concerned, it is easy enough to specify small amounts. But as yarn is not generally sold in weight measures under ¼ ounce, I specify that weight for anything from 1 to 15 yards. If you are accustomed to buying yarn by weight and have some leftover yarns, check the yard requirement where ¼ ounce is specified to see if your leftovers will suffice.

When working my own designs, how much yarn do I buy?

A trustworthy rule of thumb to use for mesh sizes 10 through 18 is to allow 2 yards of Persian yarn to the square inch.

Won't an 18 canvas use more yarn than a 10 canvas, since it has so many more stitches to the square inch?

Yes it will. But remember that for the 10 mesh you will be using a full strand of Persian yarn, whereas for the 18 mesh you will be using only one ply. On the 18 mesh, therefore, the same amount of yardage will yield three times as many strands. Thus, in rough terms, the amount needed is about the same for the canvas sizes mentioned earlier.

Is there any shortcut to estimating yarn requirements for a complicated design?

No. But it may help to place your unworked needlepoint over a 1-inch square grid made of heavy black lines. The square inches of each color will then be easier to count. An alternate method is to place a plastic sheet with a 1-inch grid on top of your unworked canvas (see the "Shopping Guide").

Is it possible to check my estimate?

I always double-check by finding my square-inch total and then doubling this figure to arrive at my total yarn count. For example, if my canvas is 10 by 10 inches, my square-inch total is 100. As I use 2 yards for each of those square inches, I double that total, arriving at a figure of 200 yards. My various color estimates—how much blue, how much red, etc.—should add up to 200 or *more*, or I have underestimated. As I much prefer to overestimate, I always allow more than is called for.

Do people use yarns differently in terms of amounts needed?

Indeed they do. Some people rip a great deal in the search for the ideal. Some use up every bit of each strand, while others leave long tails of yarn unused. Moreover, some stitches require much more yarn than others, and some designs generate a good deal of waste. You should try to take all these factors into consideration when ordering yarns.

How do you estimate rug yarns?

On a 5-mesh rug canvas, allow 1 yard of yarn for every 1½ square inches.

Do different meshes require different yarns?

Yes, and this is the special beauty of Persian yarn. Because it has three strands that pull apart so easily, Persian yarn is versatile enough to be used on any mesh from 5 to 20. On the 5 mesh you would need to use about a 7- or 8-ply strand, while a 20 mesh would use but a single strand.

Different stitches also require varying yarn amounts, so it is a good idea to try your yarn first to see if it will cover properly. Never use more than you need. A good rule of thumb to remember is that slanting stitches require *less* yarn than straight stitches.

Does the color of a yarn affect its weight or thickness?

Oddly enough, it does. Because the yarns take dyes differently, you may find that Persian yarns in certain colors are thicker and fuzzier than they are in others. I find that this difference is most significant when I am working Basketweave on a 14 mesh or Bargello on a 10 mesh. On 14 mesh I use either 1- or 2-ply strands—whichever will cover. On 10 mesh, when working Bargello, I have found that a 4-ply strand may sometimes be necessary to cover the canvas adequately.

How can I translate ounces into yards and vice versa?

Here is a conversion table:

¼ ounce	= 1–15 yards	2½ ounces	= 136–150 yards
½ ounce	= 16–30 yards	3 ounces	= 166–180 yards
¾ ounce	= 31–45 yards	4 ounces	= 226–240 yards
1 ounce	= 46–60 yards	5 ounces	= 286–300 yards
1¼ ounces	= 61–75 yards	6 ounces	= 346–360 yards
1½ ounces	= 76–90 yards	7 ounces	= 406–420 yards
1¾ ounces	= 91–105 yards	8 ounces	= 466–480 yards
2 ounces	= 106–120 yards		

I don't feel confident about selecting colors. Can you give me any hints?

Color is a matter of individual preference as well as of trial and error. Artists know that color is an enormously complex field of study, and that colors not only affect the viewer differently, but affect each other strongly. Light colors tend to advance and dark to recede. A white square on a black background will look larger than the reverse. Colors in the blue and green family are referred to as "cool," and those in the red and yellow family as "warm." These are not arbitrary designations. Experiments actually indicate that a person will feel up to 7 degrees *warmer* in a room that has been painted in warm tones, and vice versa. This means that a warm color actually stimulates blood circulation! In his wonderful and informative book, *The Elements of Color*, published by Van Nostrand Reinhold, Johannes Itten writes that sensitivity to colors is based on subjective attraction. This attraction causes people to perceive colors that they don't like as more muted than colors they find attractive. I highly recommend this book to those who would like to learn more about color and its effects on us.

Since I find it difficult to carry color in my head, is there any good way to "match" yarn colors to the design?

If you cannot bring the actual piece to be copied or worked to the yarn store, find the best color match you can from a paint chip, a fabric sample, a magazine cutout, or anything at all that will help. Bring this to the shop to assure the closest possible match.

Have you any good ideas on how to store leftover yarns? I find this a real headache.

I don't blame you for finding this difficult. It is a nuisance to have bits and pieces lying around getting tangled, and they are impossible to find or separate when needed. Moreover, wool, when left in the air for too long, tends to get a sticky feel to it and strands can cling together.

I have found that one of the best solutions is to store my yarns in large mason jars according to color. This not only keeps them tidy and airtight but allows you to see in a minute what colors you have and how much. In addition, the jars look so lovely when placed in a Welsh cupboard or along an open shelf—the reds resembling freshly canned tomatoes, the greens a batch of dill pickles, the pinks sweet cooked rhubarb, the blues . . . well, you see my drift.

CANVAS

Are there many different types of canvas?

Canvas or mesh (I use the words interchangeably) comes in many sizes that can have either double or single threads. It is usually 36 inches wide, and when I specify mesh yardage I assume this width. Some canvas does come in narrower widths, and now there is a 54-inch mono mesh that is excellent for larger projects.

Penelope. This is the name given to canvas that has a double-thread weave. This is to accommodate both very small (petit-point) and larger stitches on the same canvas. I generally do not specify this type of canvas for several reasons. While a fine make of Penelope canvas is just as strong or stronger than its single-thread counterpart, the double-thread holes are harder to see, and it's possible to inadvertently split the threads and create uneven stitches. In addition, some stitches do not cover Penelope canvas very well, so it is not recommended for either decorative stitchery or Bargello.

On the other hand, if you are planning a piece on which you would like to have two different sizes of Basketweave or Continental stitches, you must use Penelope. The double threads are split to form a tiny petit-point stitch that is half as large as the others. To my mind, however, there is no need to use Penelope canvas unless you intend to split the threads.

Mono. This canvas has a single-thread weave and clearly defined holes for working needlepoint stitches. It can be used for any type of stitch with the exception of the Half-Cross, which would pull the canvas badly out of shape. (But the Half-Cross is a stitch that I do not recommend in any case because it does not provide a suitable backing for your work.)

Do the sizes of the holes in the canvas differ?

There is a wide variety of canvas sizes to chose from. The size of hole that you select is determined by the work that is to be done. The largest size canvas that I have worked has five meshes to the inch. This double-thread canvas has very large holes, and therefore is referred to as quickpoint canvas. It is worked with rug yarn, and it is best for bold graphic designs. With only five stitches to the inch, not much detail can be incorporated into a design unless it is a very large piece. I have never seen a 5 mono mesh, but as the holes are so large, I do not mind working this size in Penelope.

There is a 7 quickpoint canvas, also Penelope, that works well with either thinner synthetic rug yarn or a 4- or 5-ply strand of Persian yarn. The 10 and 12 mono mesh are the most popular. For larger projects, the 10 will allow detail and shading. Its equivalent in Penelope mesh would be designated 10/20, because by splitting the double threads you would get twenty stitches to the inch. The 12 mesh is the most versatile. It is large enough to prevent eye strain and small enough to allow substantial subtlety of design. The 14 mesh is also quite popular and allows finer shading. And then there is a 16, an 18, a 20, and so on up to a silk canvas of 40 holes to the inch and even higher.

What is petit-point?

Opinions may differ, but generally needlepoint that is worked on a 16 mesh or even finer canvas is called petit-point due to the small size of the stitch.

How do I decide which mesh to use for my projects?

This will depend on three major factors: the size and the complexity of the finished work and the state of your eyes. If you wish to trace a highly complex design for a pillow or a vest—one that has many curved lines and subtle shading—a 14 mesh or higher would be indicated. Curved lines are hard to form on a small project with few holes to the inch. The square holes of needlepoint can never actually shape circles, but with a large enough number of stitches, one can create the *illusion* of circles. The smaller stitches that are possible with the finer canvases allow more detail to be incorporated. The use of large mesh suggests a large project.

Let's suppose you wish to work a graphed design for which a small mesh (14 or 16) is suggested, but you find it easier and more comfortable to work on a 10 mesh. There is no reason why you cannot do this effectively—as long as the *increase* in the total size is acceptable to you. A graphed design that would work out to a total size of 12 by 12 inches on a 14 mesh, will be a bit under a 17-inch square on a 10 mesh.

Or perhaps you must have a gift ready on short notice, and the design you wish to trace is a large simple flower with bold colors and a small amount of shading. In this case, you could select a 5 quickpoint canvas and have your pillow needlepointed and ready for mounting in less than a week.

In general, a 12 mesh is the most versatile size for a pillow. It is not so small a hole that it is difficult to see and time-consuming to work, but neither is it so large a hole that it will not accommodate itself to some nice detail and soft shading.

The point to remember is that the most complex and intricate work can be done on large mesh as long as the total size of the finished piece is large enough to allow all the details to be worked in. For this reason, many rugs are worked on a 10 mesh.

Do different meshes require different yarns?

Yes, and this is the beauty of Persian yarns. As the Persian yarn is made up of 3-ply strands that easily pull apart, it is versatile enough to be used on any mesh from a 5 to a 20.

Varying stitches may require different ply even on the same canvas. It is always a good idea to try your yarn and stitch first to see if it will cover properly. Never use more than you need or your work will look bulky and your holes will get pulled out of shape. Because slanting stitches cover an intersection of both vertical and horizontal canvas threads in one stroke, less yarn can be used for this type of stitch. A straight stitch lies flat between two parallel canvas threads, and the threads may show if the yarn is not fat enough.

Is mesh available only in white?

No, mesh comes in ecru, olive green, and a yellowish shade as well. Some people prefer this colored mesh because they find it easier on their eyes and they feel that the yarns will cover better than on a pure white surface. This would pertain to graphed or traced designs, or any work done on blank canvas. I find Pulled-Thread stitches look very well on an ecru canvas, but in general, I prefer the white because I can balance my colors better against a white background.

Are there any special types of canvas?

There is a type called mustarmesh, which is a 54-inch wide soft ecru Penelope canvas with a design *woven* right into it in white. The designs are usually small repeats. Because the designs can be worked in any colors you choose, they provide a wide range of diversity despite the fixed patterns. The wide width also makes this type excellent for large chair seats and backs.

Is there any way to tell good canvas from bad?

Buy good quality or you will be sorry later. Cotton or linen mesh is best. It should be stiff but a bit silky to the touch. The firmness of good canvas will remain until you are done working. Bad-quality canvas will lose all its stiffness in handling, it will curl away from you, and the holes will become impossible to find. Your stitches will pull the holes out of shape, and the result of much effort will be a work that is difficult, uneven, and distorted. Your best guarantee of good canvas is to buy the best quality you can find even though it costs more. It will be worth it in the end.

How do I cut the mesh?

You need a 2-inch border of raw canvas all the way around your design area for ease of blocking later on. This translates to a total of 4 inches added to both dimensions before you cut. For instance, if your chair seat measures 10 by 15 inches, you should cut your canvas to at least 14 by 19 inches. Use a large pair of sharp scissors and cut straight along a "track" between two canvas threads.

After I have cut it, will the canvas fray at the edges?

Yes, unless you are working with a lock-weave canvas. This type is somewhat stiffer and less silky than the others, but it holds its shape beautifully and will not fray. If you are not using this type of canvas, be sure to bind the edges of your mesh with masking tape that is at least ½ inches wide, or work a zigzag stitch around the edges of the canvas on your sewing machine. You can also turn the edges under ½ inch and sew them down with a straight stitch.

Should I work one part of the canvas before another?

In general it is best to either work from the center out or work the design and then the background, but this is not a hard and fast rule and pertains mostly to projects worked in Basketweave or Continental. It is always a good idea to work all outlines before filling in, however. This gives you the opportunity to see if a given line is shaping up as you wish it to, before the bulk of the work is added. This is very important with curved lines and geometric forms.

SUPPLIES

Needlepoint basically requires only four ingredients: a needle, canvas, yarn, and a scissors. This is why it is so easy to take with you when traveling, visiting the doctor's office, or going anyplace where you expect to have leisure time.

When working needlepoint, must I have many supplies on hand?

For reproducing designs, graph paper and tracing paper are most helpful. A pencil you surely will have. A heavy-duty stapler and a plywood board a bit larger than your needlepoint are needed for blocking. A clear acrylic fixative spray (available at art supply stores) will keep your pencil lines from smudging and discoloring the yarns. Waterproof marking pens are also helpful (see "Marking Canvas").

What is the best type of scissors to use for needlepoint?

Any small 4- to 6-inch sharp-pointed scissors will do. The sharp point is important for ripping, although some people prefer to use the curved blade of a seam-ripper, which is available at most sewing and dressmaker supply shops. I am lost without my chatelaine, a decorative ribbon or measuring tape to which my favorite scissors is attached. I wear this draped around my neck for easy access when working. Otherwise I continually lose or misplace my scissors. For cutting your canvas, use a large dressmaker's shears.

Should I use a frame, and if so, when?

A floor frame can be a lovely addition to the furniture of any room. If I were working a room-sized rug, I would use one. It is slow going because the needle must be pulled through to the back after each stitch instead of coming forward in the same motion to start the next stitch. But it would hold the weight of the canvas and guarantee that my stitches would be even with no telltale lines running across the background. In addition, the canvas would suffer no distortion at all. A smaller, roll-type frame is excellent for Pulled-Thread stitch work to keep the tension even. There are several very useful types of frame-holders, some that rest on a tabletop, others that you can sit on to hold in place, and others that rest on your lap.

It may also be a good idea to use frames when a number of people—such as church or synagogue groups—are sharing the work of one large project and where each needlepointer is likely to exert a different tension on one section of a mural.

I have had the experience of trying to piece together the work of about fifteen different women to form an exquisite religious wall-hanging. As most of the segments had been worked in the Continental stitch, it proved to be an almost insurmountable problem for me! The distortion was so great that the only possible solution was to mount the entire work on plywood, stretching it mercilessly back into something of its former shape. It turned out to be an object of great beauty and artistry, of which the women who had worked on it and I were very proud!

Are there any vision aids that might help me to do fine work?

There are several types of magnifiers and high-intensity lamps that are recommended. Some magnifiers tie around your neck and rest on your chest, requiring no holding. Another type, which comes in three different magnification intensities, clips right onto your eyeglasses. Then there are several floor and table model goose-neck lamps with high-intensity lights and magnifiers. All of these are excellent for working petit-point, or if your eyesight is poor.

9

MARKING CANVAS

What shall I use to mark the canvas?

When tracing, I am dreadfully wary of almost everything except pencils, and even these may show through on light yarns if not sprayed with a clear acrylic fixative. Most markers, even those called "permanent," tend to bleed if you wet your canvas, as you will do when blocking. The only one I have come to trust is the AD Marker in #3 warm gray permanent. These are manufactured by Cooper Color Inc., Jacksonville, Florida. If you wish to try other colors or other makes, use only those marked permanent and test them first. Check each color by scribbling a small area of color on a scrap of canvas. Let it dry and then put the canvas under running water. If *any* color comes off, don't use the marker. If the color does not come off, let the canvas dry and then check again for bleeding. If your color outlines have remained absolutely stable, with no fuzzing around the edges, your marker has passed the test. If your marker does not pass the test, you can try again—this time spraying your design with acrylic fixative. Use a marker *only* if there is no bleeding or running.

What is the best type of pencil to use?

The harder the pencil lead, the less likely it is to come off on your yarn. But a hard pencil is very difficult to see on canvas. A medium pencil is therefore the best. "H" signifies hard, "B" is soft, and "HB" is medium. Where numbers are used, the lower the number the harder the pencil. A #2 is a medium.

I have heard that pencil is bad for the canvas. Is this true?

I too have read that graphite will deteriorate canvas, but I have not found this to be true. Nonetheless, I use no more markings on my canvas than are strictly necessary.

PAINTING CANVAS

If I wish to paint my own canvases, what shall I use to do so?

It is harder than it appears to paint your own canvases, but if you wish to do so it is best to work with acrylic paint. This is water soluble, dries quickly, and is fully waterproof when dry. Oil paints have lovely clear colors, but unless they are mixed with a drying agent, they may take months to dry completely.

TRACING DESIGNS

How do you recommend tracing designs on to canvas?

This can usually be done, simply and easily, by placing your canvas directly over the design to be traced. However, if you are using a very fine mesh and the many threads obscure your vision, or if you are copying something from a book that is too cramped to copy easily, it might be better to trace your design first on tracing paper or tissue paper with a good heavy Magic Marker. Then place your canvas on top of this. The heavy lines should make your design easier to see under the canvas.

You need not be perfectly accurate when tracing unless you are trying to copy a precise geometric form. In that case you should *not* trace at all, but should graph your design. Needlepoint mesh never will hold exactly straight, and a geometric form is sure to be uneven if traced. Remember also that your mesh is made up of squares, and you can never truly reproduce a rounded line. Do the best you can, and the eye of the beholder will do the rest. The smaller the mesh, the better the illusion of curves will be.

What do I do about transferring color on to the mesh?

In general, it is not necessary to transfer color. Simply keep the original design beside you as you work and refer to it for color. If you cannot keep the original, make a tracing of it and mark the areas of color with key numbers or letters to serve as a reference. If your dark yarns will not cover some areas of white mesh, it may be necessary to cover these areas with a wash of acrylic color.

When tracing designs on to mesh, where should I begin?

Hold the canvas very taut and very straight over your design. Then start with the outlines and work toward your general effect. Correct your proportions first, and add small details later.

GRAPHING DESIGNS

Instead of tracing, can I graph my own designs or others?

Yes you can, and it is especially important to do so if you wish to copy an exact geometric form. The design should be worked out first on graph paper. Sometimes, particularly with rounded forms, it is best to then try out your graphed design on a scrap of mesh to see if the shape is what you envisioned. To graph designs other than geometrics, you might use the Ultragraph, or a similar device. This consists of a large clear acetate sheet that has been ruled with ten, twelve, fourteen, or five squares to the inch. You place this over your design, then trace the design on the acetate with a special marking pen that can later be erased. The "Shopping Guide" at the back of this book will tell you where you can obtain the Ultragraph.

PROBLEMS AND REMEDIES

Are all yarn dyes colorfast?

The French Persian yarns have proved to be completely colorfast. For many years the Paterna yarns were, too, but new federal government regulations designed to protect the environment have affected the methods used to dye yarns in the United States. Therefore, certain dyes, notably dark reds and deep blues, may tend to bleed if soaked in water. Test these colors first. Generally your needlepoint is completely washable, but if you find bleeding, it would be best to have your piece dry-cleaned. You can moisten the back of the canvas without soaking completely through during the blocking process. If your yarns bleed badly, use a steam iron for blocking.

If I get a "painted" canvas and am unsure if it is colorfast, what should I do?

By all means test the color by thoroughly wetting a small corner of your piece and letting it dry. If *any* color runs off, or if outlines become fuzzy when it is dry, do not use it. Your canvas will lose its sizing when wet, but you can bring back some of its original stiffness by stapling it to a board until dry again.

If I design my own canvas, how can I be sure there will be no discoloration or bleeding problems?

If you are using a pencil, spray it with a clear acrylic fixative to be sure it does not come off on light-colored yarns. If you are using Magic Markers, carefully test them by marking a piece of scrap canvas, wetting it down completely, and allowing it to dry thoroughly. No color should come off, and all outlines should remain crystal clear. To be extra sure, use acrylic spray. If you are painting, use acrylic paints.

If you wish to use oils, mix with a quick-drying agent or small amount of white enamel and test for time of total dryness before starting out.

Loose ends of yarn left to dangle in back of your work may well be drawn to the front with subsequent stitches. This can discolor certain areas. Your light yarns will pick up dark shadows, and your dark yarns will be flecked with lighter fluff. Be sure, therefore, to weave your loose ends through the stitches in the back, and then snip the ends off close to your canvas. This will not only keep your canvas from discoloring, but it will also keep lumpy spots from forming.

Is there an "art" to ripping?

Yes, of sorts. It has always seemed unfair that ripping is harder than any needlepoint stitch, and the hardest stitch to rip is the basic Basketweave or Continental. The great danger when ripping is that you will cut your canvas, and if you do this you are in real trouble. So rip carefully and slowly. Start on the reverse side, using the point of your scissors to pull the yarn up and away from the canvas, toward you. Before you cut, make sure that you do not have any canvas on the scissors. Then do the same on the right side of the canvas, plucking at the back to pull away the cut ends of stitches. Keep repeating this process, working first on the back and then on the front of your canvas, until the desired area is free to rework.

What should I do if I cut the canvas?

Don't cry, first of all. It's difficult to fix but not impossible. Clear an area around the cut portion so the canvas has no worked stitches for about six uncut threads all around. Using strong white sewing thread or dental floss—not yarn—weave in and out of the existing canvas threads, going under and over the canvas mesh to reproduce the original weave. Start some distance away from the cut, anchoring your yarn around an intersection of canvas threads. Go back and forth with your thread until it forms a weave almost as thick as the original canvas. In essence you are just darning. Although the result may not look much like your canvas threads, if you have woven the thread under and over properly, your stitches will work neatly on to it and no one will notice the rip.

What can you do if decorative stitches do not fit correctly at the sides of the work or around the central design?

You must compensate. This means you must form a stitch which, without losing the essential pattern of the stitch, will adapt to the space left to it. A compensating stitch is always smaller than the original stitch.

If you find that you require so much compensating that your pattern will constantly be tortured beyond recognition, simply work the Continental or Basketweave around your central design, or around your far edges. I have done this around the flowers in the Floral Fabric Pillow on page 121.

I have worked a large area of my needlepoint, and now find that my dark background yarn has not covered properly and white mesh shows through. What shall I do?

Here is a remedy that I find works very nicely. Take a single ply of Persian yarn, or any strand of the same color yarn, and, using a needle, pull it right under a horizontal row of stitches. Do one row after the other in this manner. These strands need not be anchored if you snip off the ends carefully.

When working on a blank canvas, how can I prevent the white from showing through?

If you are worried about this happening, and sometimes it does no matter how well you try to cover, then paint on an acrylic wash in a lighter shade of the yarn color. Allow it to dry before working.

I have worked a good bit of my needlepoint, and find that the holes that are left have all started to crush together. What shall I do?

This happens for one of two reasons. If you are using a low quality of canvas, the holes will easily pull out of shape. The best way to avoid this is to start in the center and work out. The other reason is that you may be using too heavy a yarn. Sometimes on a 14 mesh, one strand will not fully cover, but two strands pulls the holes out of shape. My remedy for this is to alternately use first a 2-ply and then a 1-ply strand. This does not show, and keeps the holes from distorting. It is also helpful to work from the center out.

I bought what I realize now must be a silk-screened rather than a hand-painted canvas, and I find that the design lines on either side are not straight. What should I do?

Due to the fact that needlepoint mesh is never exactly straight, only laborious counting can ensure a straight line. This is why hand-painted canvases, and particularly geometrics, are frequently quite expensive. They are well worth it! But if you have run into a problem with a silk-screened canvas, remember it is best to always work your outlines, straight lines, and curved lines first. This way you can pick up any mistakes, straighten out uneven lines, align all small repeats, and get the best-looking circles. You may find that you are completely reorganizing the design and working green yarn over red paint, etc., but don't worry.

It is especially important to work lettering first to be sure it fits properly into the space allotted to it and that sufficient space is allowed between each letter.

If I wish to work two identical pieces of canvas, or if I wish to begin a large project consisting of twelve bird canvases that will later be joined together, is there anything I should be wary of at this point?

Two things. One is to be absolutely sure that the selvedge edges of your canvas are on the same side of each piece. If the pieces you are purchasing have the selvedge edge removed, ask for a new set to be made up to ensure uniformity or you will have a terrible time when you try to line up your finished sections. Needlepoint holes may look square, but they are not. One dimension is microscopically longer than the other, and this tiny disparity, multiplied by the number of holes on your canvas can add up to a rather large total.

Also, if the project will take a long time to complete (perhaps a few years) then don't work your background until you have finished all your central motifs. Then buy all your background yarn at once. In this way you will avoid the problem of dye-lot changes, uneven aging of your yarn, or stitching differences. Yarn does fade with time, and a large project may take years to complete.

My colors ran when I had my needlepoint blocked, and now the work is a mess. What can I do?

Oh dear. Almost nothing, except rip. I have tried soaking the piece in cold water and then beating it against the side of a tub. This does take out some of the discoloration, but not all. Only ripping and reworking will cure the condition completely.

I have worked a canvas that I love, but now I am afraid that perhaps the colors are not fast. What shall I do? It is out of shape and badly needs blocking.

When you bring it in to be blocked, tell those who will be working on it that you wish it to be steam blocked. Or you can do the blocking yourself. Use a steam iron and a damp cloth on the wrong side of your work, and repeatedly press your piece while pulling it strongly back into shape.

I know you once wrote a book for lefties, but this book does not have instructions for lefties. How can I use it if I am left-handed?

Poor lefties! You are really an underprivileged minority. The costs of publishing prohibit another leftie book, but I did experiment with this one and find that you should turn the book so that the left-hand edge is on the bottom—a 90 degree turn. The diagrams should work for you, and from this position you can still read the instructions if necessary. In most cases, the diagrams are so explicit that text may not even be required. Where you do need some explanation, you need only amend the text so that where it reads "Bring your yarn over to the *right* over four canvas threads," you will see from the way you are holding the diagram that you are bringing your yarn *up* over four canvas threads. For stitches that are worked on all sides, such as the Algerian Eye, the Diamond Eye, and the Cross-Box, you can work directly from the text with the diagrams upright just as right-handers would. I hope this is a help. Good luck!

My canvas design was painted right to the edge, and that is how I have needlepointed it. Can it be blocked?

Yes, but with great difficulty and not the same effect. In the future, do not buy a canvas that does not give you a good-sized border of raw canvas all the way around the design. You need this area for stapling and pulling when blocking. Lacking it, your canvas will have to be steam blocked. You can do this yourself with a steam iron. Moisten your canvas from the back, place a damp cloth over it, and then press. Keep pulling it back into shape as you press.

I spilled coffee on my canvas, and now the canvas has lost its stiffness. What shall I do?

If you spilled coffee on a *completed* canvas, you would have to put it in cold water with a cold-water soap, and wash it without rubbing. Just pull it up and down in the water until the stain is out. Then staple your finished canvas to a plywood board and allow it to dry thoroughly. If you have spilled something on an unworked canvas, then you need not wash it. Just staple the piece to a board to dry, and work right over the stain. If you are afraid that the stain will come out in later blocking, however, it is best to wash it before stapling it to the board.

If I soil my needlepoint, can it be washed?

Yes, as described above, needlepoint can be thoroughly immersed in cool water with a soap used for woolens. Do not rub, and do not wring. Roll the wet canvas in a towel when washed to take out the excess moisture, and then block. If it has already been blocked, just stretch it on a towel to dry. Needlepoint worked in metallics, cotton, and wool can go right into the washing machine and dryer. I would have silks and velvet yarn dry-cleaned.

STITCHES

How do I know how many plies of yarn to use for different stitches?

You really have to experiment to find which weight and type of yarn looks best on any particular canvas. It is worthwhile to work a practice area first at the edge of your piece or on a scrap of canvas. You should never use more yarn than you need to cover the canvas or your work will look bulky, holes may be forced together, and decorative stitches may lose their definition. Slanting or diagonal stitches require less yarn than straight up-and-down stitches. Patterns that have a great many stitches in their formation, such as the Algerian Eye or Cross-Box, will use less ply. The "eye" stitches generally use only a 1-ply strand as they keep returning to the same hole with each stitch in the formation. The Smyrna Double-Cross stitch and the Rice stitch tend to lose all definition if worked with too much yarn.

Are there a great many different types of stitches?

There are hundreds. The international and historical character of needlepoint becomes apparent if you study the names of some of the many stitches: Parisian, Greek, Scotch, Algerian Eye, Byzantine, Milanese, Smyrna Double-Cross, Turkey Knot, and French Knot.

Each of these stitches forms a distinctive pattern that can be mixed with others, enlarged, or miniaturized.

But is there one basic stitch?

In a sense, yes. The basic needlepoint stitch, that simple small diagonal stitch that reaches up and over one intersection of vertical and horizontal threads, is the stitch that is most familiar. Although it always looks the same on the front of the canvas, it has several names: the Half-Cross, the Continental, and the Basketweave stitch. Its generic name is the Tent stitch, undoubtedly because it leans up diagonally like the side of a tent.

If these stitches all look the same on the front of the canvas, what differentiates them?

The Continental is worked in a horizontal line from the right side of your canvas to the left. It forms an excellent backing and is the most useful and versatile of the Tent stitches, but it pulls the canvas badly out of shape and needs to be turned upside-down every other row, which is a great nuisance.

The Basketweave is worked in diagonal rows starting at the upper right-hand corner. It gives the best of all backings to your canvas, creates hardly any canvas distortion, and never needs to be turned. It can only be used for concentrated areas of color and not on single lines, however, so it is not as versatile as the Continental. It may also leave faint diagonal lines showing in a large area of one color. An additional drawback is that it is hard for some people to learn, although it is truly not hard at all to *do*. It derives its name from the basketweave pattern that is formed on the back side of your canvas.

The Half-Cross is a form of Tent stitch that is seldom useful. It is worked in a horizontal row from left to right and gives no backing whatever to your canvas. It also pulls your mesh badly out of shape and needs to be turned every other row. The only reason that I can think of for using the Half-Cross is to save yarn. (The yarn that is *not* covering the back of your canvas is saved.)

How will I decide which stitch to use?

Each stitch has its own advantages and disadvantages. Some lie flat, and others stand high. Some do not cover the back of your canvas and, therefore, will not take a great deal of wear. Some are made up of small tight stitches, others of loose loopy ones that might catch on a sharp object if used on a chair seat or eyeglass case. Some will compensate easily, and others only with the greatest of difficulty. Accompanying the diagrams and directions for each stitch in this book is a short discussion of the qualities of that stitch and its relative ease of compensation. When making your selection, you should take all these factors into consideration, as well as your subjective liking of a stitch. In general, the best-wearing stitch is the Basketweave, but you will find that you have favorites in the decorative stitches as well. One of my greatest favorites is the Smyrna Double-Cross, which I used as the background stitch for my Harper's Lady. For speed and ease, the Brick stitch is tops. For a fabulous high-textured border, there is nothing like the Cross-Box stitch, though it's a nuisance to work! Try them all, and find your own favorite.

What exactly is compensation?

You will frequently find that a decorative stitch does not fit perfectly into your working area. This may occur because you wish to work it around an uneven central motif, or because it does not form a straight edge along the side of your work. In either case, your stitch pattern must be adapted to fit the available space, without losing its essential formation. These adapted stitches are called compensating stitches. A compensating stitch is always *smaller* than the stitch in the original pattern. It can never be larger. Many of the stitch diagrams show how compensation is accomplished under a variety of circumstances.

When two stitches share the same hole, should the second stitch start or end in the shared hole?

It is always best to start a stitch from an unoccupied hole and move to the occupied hole so you don't risk splitting the yarn already in that hole. This is the expert's rule, although I have occasionally felt it would be helpful to the beginner to have a firm starting point, and I have advised starting in an occupied hole.

Do the decorative stitches pull your work out of shape?

They generally do not. A few, such as the Scotch or the Byzantine, which are made up of enlarged versions of the Continental, may pull your canvas a bit out of shape, but not too badly.

FINISHING TOUCHES

How—and why—should I block my finished work?

Blocking gives a more finished appearance to your work even if it has not been pulled out of shape. It gets the stitches back into line. If you have used high decorative stitches and don't want them to flatten out, block your canvas face-up. Otherwise, block it face-down after wetting it thoroughly. To block, first staple your wet canvas to a clean plywood board. Keep canvas edges as straight as possible. Start stapling at one corner and work across, pulling hard as you go. Move around your canvas, stapling it down securely, until your work is squarely and firmly anchored to the plywood. Leave the canvas on the board until completely dry (overnight or usually longer). Now it is ready to be mounted.

Can I mount the finished needlepoint myself?

The word "mount" means to put your stitched needlepoint into its final form. Many pillows can be mounted by amateur stitchers who are good with a sewing machine. I do not include myself among these and invariably take my work to a professional. If you have some skill at hand-sewing, a simple piped or unpiped pillow is not hard to make. Most home sewing machines will rebel if asked to work through velvet piping, velvet backing, and needlepointed canvas, so it might be best to make a simple unpiped knife-edged pillow if you plan to back it with a heavy fabric. Adding fringe to a pillow is exquisite; piping lends a finished border, especially to box-edged pillows; and setting a small needlepoint into a piece of fabric like a plaque and then mounting it into a pillow is lovely. But all of these I feel should be left to the experts. I certainly would not attempt a vest unless I were an experienced dressmaker.

But if you still want to try your hand, I have given instructions in the "Blocking and Finishing" chapter.

What filling should be used for pillows?

I used to use only down until it became very expensive. If you want almost the ultimate in luxury and hang the expense, then specify 60 percent to 40 percent down and feathers. I now use a high grade of kapok for the inner pillow form. It is soft, light, and not a bit lumpy.

Should I have my mounted work dry-cleaned?

Yes. Send your vest or pillows to be dry-cleaned. With pillows, be sure to tell the dry cleaner what filler you have used, as some cleaning fluids may deteriorate these. You might also make your pillow with a zipper so the inner cushion can be removed before cleaning.

PART ONE
STITCHES

Introduction to Stitches

It has been my experience that even the most imaginative and informative stitchery books give the reader only the briefest of stitch descriptions and one or two photographs or diagrams as teaching aids. This often creates difficulties even for the most advanced stitchers. Therefore, I have attempted to present as many diagrams with every stitch as seemed necessary for a full grasp of the intricacies and potential difficulties. In some cases I have also added a few variations of a particular stitch for the more adventuresome.

The following stitches are all used in one or more of the projects described. I have arranged them in alphabetical sequence for easy access.

Do not hesitate to experiment with these stitch forms—combine them, distort them, and try for different effects through the unusual use of color. Remember that needlepoint is a changing and ever-developing art form that is flexible and creative. This is both the challenge and the source of great satisfaction and pleasure that needlepoint brings.

Algerian Eye

This stitch belongs to the family of "pulled" stitches—so called because after each stitch the yarn is given a little pull or tug in a deliberate effort to pull the canvas out of shape. In this case, we want the central eye to open wide. It is a painful figure of speech, but when working the Algerian Eye formation, keep in mind that your needle must always go into the eye, not emerge from it.

The Algerian Eye is a lovely border stitch, but almost impossible to compensate successfully. It can be made wider or narrower where the design demands, but the difference will surely show. It is an excellent stitch to use wherever a square shape is called for.

As you must go in and out of the central eye so many times, use a single ply of yarn on almost any size canvas. This stitch, as shown, covers an area of four-by-four canvas threads, but it can be worked in any size— larger or smaller—and over an odd or even number of canvas threads.

1. Bring the needle out through the center top of your stitch (shown here as the darkened hole), straight down two canvas threads into the shaded hole or eye, and emerge one hole to the left. Give your yarn a little tug as you emerge to widen the eye. When working this stitch, it is important that your yarn be properly anchored in back or you will not get good tension. The tension will remain quite firm if you weave the yarn through the back of your work—first in a direction away from where you will start your Algerian Eye, and then back again. If you have no finished work through which to weave the yarn, then hold about an inch of the yarn "tail" firmly in back in such a way that your next stitches will cover it, splice it, and anchor it.

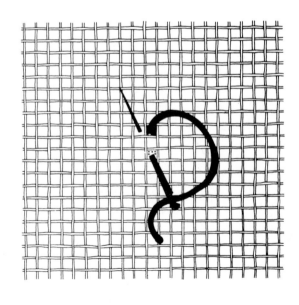

2. Push your needle through the shaded eye, again emerging one hole to the left of the darkened hole, and give a little tug.

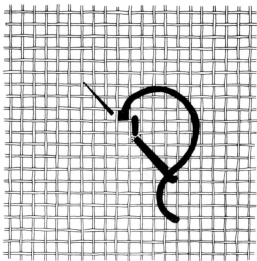

3. Push the needle through the shaded eye; but now, because you have reached your first corner, you will emerge *under* the darkened hole. Remember to tug.

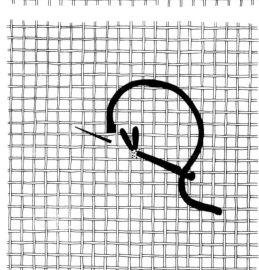

4. Once again, go into the eye, emerge under the darkened hole, and give a little tug. Continue in this manner for three more stitches. The third stitch will signal that you have reached another corner.

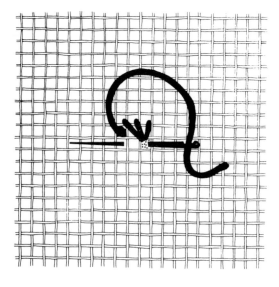

5. The Algerian Eye formation covers four-by-four canvas threads, so you have reached your lower left-hand corner when four horizontal canvas threads are covered. Here the stitch has reached the corner, so after putting your needle through the eye, emerge immediately to the *right* of the darkened hole to begin forming the bottom part of your square. Repeat the stitches until you have reached your lower right-hand corner, when four vertical canvas threads are covered. As you complete this corner stitch, you will bring your needle into the eye and emerge one hole *above* your last stitch before giving a tug.

6. Here we see the Algerian Eye nearing the upper right-hand corner. When it reaches this corner, the needle will go into the eye, emerge one hole to the *left*, and go back into the eye one last time with a good tug in an upward direction.

7. Here is the Algerian Eye formation correctly completed. Pull the leftover yarn upward so the eye, which has been carefully formed by repeated tugs, is not obscured. If this motif is to stand alone, anchor the yarn above the Algerian Eye to keep tension on the strand. If you are planning a row of Algerian Eyes, you might start another either above this one, or along the top border to the right or to the left, but . . .

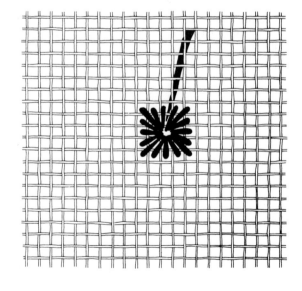

8. You must *not* start another Algerian Eye *below* this one—or allow your yarn to be anchored in a downward direction—because you will close the eye and entirely lose the proper effect.

Basketweave

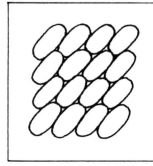

Ah, the Basketweave—easy to do but a terror to teach. This stitch is no more than a variation of the basic Tent or Continental stitch. The reverse side of the stitching resembles basketweaving, hence its name. On the front of your canvas the stitches look the same as the Continental or the Half-Cross, but the Basketweave is slightly neater and more well-defined in appearance, and it will not pull your canvas out of shape as the others most certainly will. It also provides a sturdy backing for the canvas. A major advantage is that it does not require turning your canvas at the end of each row. The Basketweave and Continental use more yarn than the Half-Cross, because the latter leaves the reverse side of your canvas almost totally exposed, giving it minimum durability.

The Basketweave is the stitch of experts. It has only two drawbacks. The first is that you cannot do a single line of Basketweave, but need a solid area of canvas to work. If your design requires working a single line or darting here and there for an odd stitch, use the Continental. Another problem is that faint diagonal lines may appear across your work when a large area is filled in with one color. In cases where an exceptionally large area is to be worked in one color, use a frame if you feel these faint lines will bother you

Do learn to work this stitch, You will love doing it, as its easy rhythm becomes almost hypnotic.

---

1. Begin in the upper right-hand corner of your design or area being worked. Bring the needle out through the darkened hole and, slanting to the right, up and over one intersection of the canvas threads. Be sure that this first intersection has a horizontal mesh thread on top (you will see why when you get to Diagram 11). Work one small slanting stitch and emerge to the left of the darkened hole. After this first starter stitch, you will begin to work upward and downward in diagonal rows. (If your design begins over a vertical thread, start work from Diagram 3, ignoring top two stitches.)

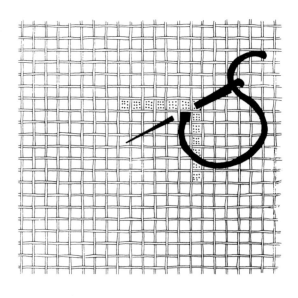

2. Work a second stitch, this time over the intersection with a vertical thread on top of the horizontal mesh thread, and emerge two canvas threads straight down into the first empty hole below the starter stitch.

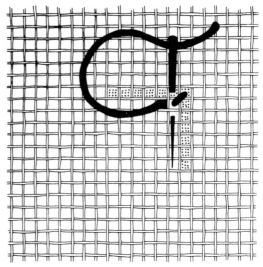

3. Work a third stitch. The shaded area is your border, and a cardinal rule to remember when learning the Basketweave is that your needle *must* always go into your border *twice*. Here you see the needle going in once and emerging beneath the darkened hole. It is now in position to work a small slanted stitch up into the border a *second* time. When you touch your border the first time, you are in effect ending your row. When you touch the border for the second time, you are *beginning* your next row. If you are not careful to do this, your work will have gaps at the side and at the top where stitches have been omitted. Many beginners have discovered this, to their sorrow, so be warned that this is the place where most mistakes are made.

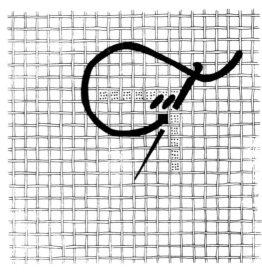

4. Here we see the needle going into the border for the second time, which indicates a change of direction. You will now be working *up* your diagonal row. From now until you reach your top border, you will be covering *only* intersections with a horizontal thread on top. After completing each small slanted stitch over this type of intersection, place your needle in a horizontal position, reach behind two canvas threads to the left, and emerge through the first empty hole.

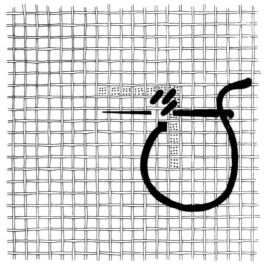

5. Again, work a stitch across the intersection with a horizontal thread on top, place your needle in a horizontal position, reach behind two canvas threads straight left, and emerge through the first empty hole. Note, as a memory aid, that when your needle is pointing horizontally, you are covering intersections with a horizontal thread on top.

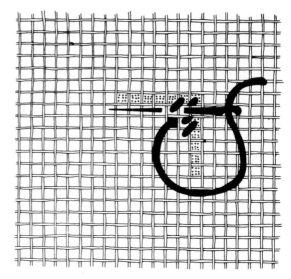

6. Again work your small slanted stitch, but see what has happened. The needle has gone into the top border once, so now you must do this again. Note how you get into position by slanting immediately to the left.

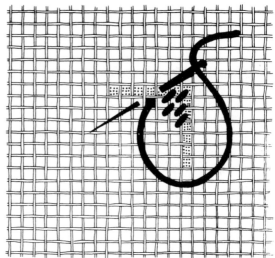

7. When you hit the border a second time, you are ready to change direction. Now you will cover only intersections that have a vertical top thread, and after each stitch you will place your needle in a vertical position, reach straight down behind two canvas threads, and emerge through the first empty hole.

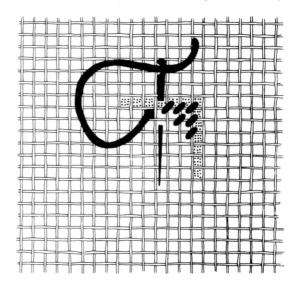

8. Continue working down your diagonal row until you hit the border. Then work back up again.

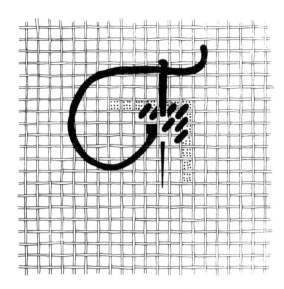

9. Each time you reach a border, emerge in such a way that your next stitch will hit the border *again*, and then change direction. You will move *up* the diagonal rows (stitching across the horizontal top threads) if your previous row moved down. Conversely, you will move *down* a diagonal row (covering vertical top threads) if your previous row went up. If you know you are moving up a diagonal, but the intersection you are about to stitch over has a vertical thread on top, you have made a mistake somewhere. Go back and check your work. Have you hit the border twice? Have you reached behind two straight canvas threads, or did you inadvertently reach behind three? These are the most common mistakes. Also check to make sure that your needle has moved either *straight* down behind the canvas (on a downward row) or *straight* left behind the canvas (on an upward row) after each stitch.

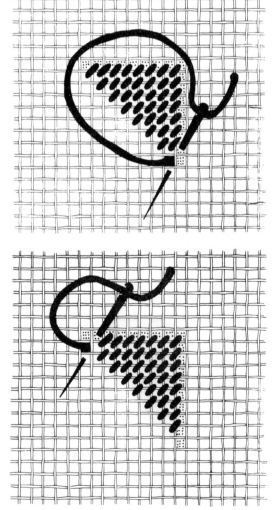

10. If, due to the shape of your design area, you reach the top border and cannot touch it again, then simply touch your *side* border for a second time. Similarly, if you have reached your side border and cannot touch it again because you have run out of room, touch your bottom border twice. *Some* border must be touched twice to signal the completion of one row and the start of the next!

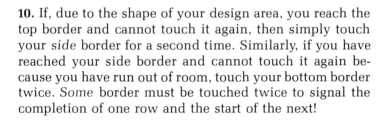

11. When working the Basketweave as a background around a central design, you can run your yarn along the *back* of a small design area, weaving it in and out of the stitches in back, and emerge a short distance away ready to pick up the rhythm of your stitches. Do not do this, however, if the distance is much more than an inch; the back of your work will become too thick and matted. In those cases, finish one row and then begin again on the other side of your design. But do be sure that you are covering vertical top thread intersections on your way down diagonal rows, when your needle is pointing straight down (vertically) between each stitch to point the way. And be sure that you are covering horizontal top thread intersections on your way up the diagonal rows, when your needle will point straight to the left (horizontally).

There are two reasons for covering the proper intersection when working your diagonal rows. The first is that your yarn will cover the canvas better. But the second is even more important. Working in this way you can never inadvertently work two adjacent diagonal rows in the same direction (for example, two up rows or two down rows), which would cause a definite ridge to appear on your work. Even if you begin work in two widely separated areas, you know that when the two areas meet, they will not—cannot—meet as two diagonal rows moving in the same direction and form a disfiguring ridge.

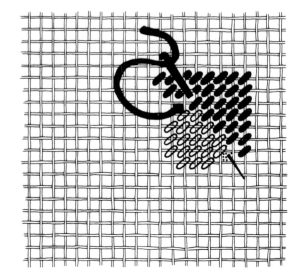

Binding

This stitch forms a neat border for your work. It is not so much a decorative stitch as a finishing stitch that helps keep your turned-back canvas edges neat in appearance.

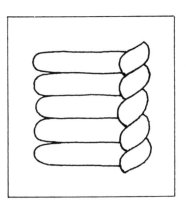

1. Fold back the edge of your canvas, leaving as many canvas threads showing as will be used in working your stitch. Be sure that the area folded back is as large or larger than the area to be worked with the Binding stitch. Note that one hole will form the bent edge and the other holes should line up exactly under those on top.

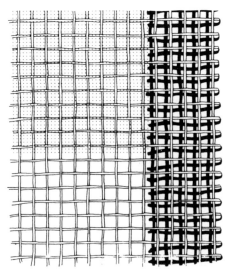

2. The dotted area indicates your finished needlepoint. The Binding stitch in this diagram will cover five mesh threads. Hold about an inch of your tail end of yarn in back of the bent edge of mesh. Now run your needle down through two layers of mesh, sharing a hole with your finished needlepoint, and emerge through the loop of yarn formed. Do not run your needle into the hole at the bend but through both layers of mesh and into the loop.

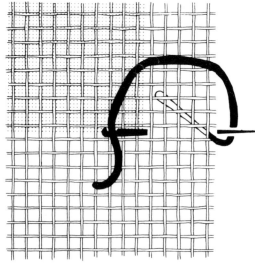

3. Once again, go through the next hole up. Again share a hole with your finished needlepoint. Your needle goes from the front of the canvas to the back, through two layers of canvas. Again bring your needle through the loop of yarn that is formed to make another knot along the bent edge of canvas.

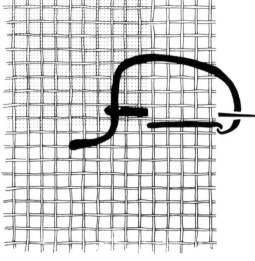

4. Continue in this manner.

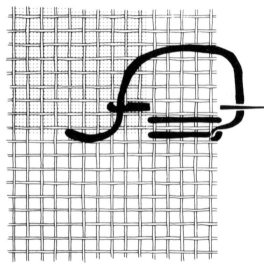

5. Be sure your knot sits right on the bent edge to form a neat braid.

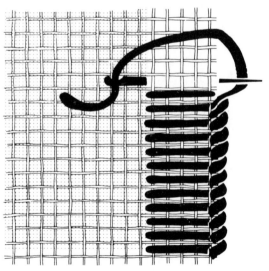

6. This is a whip-stitch variation of the Binding stitch. Fold the canvas back as before, this time coming forward to the front of your canvas through two layers, sharing a hole with your finished needlepoint. Bring your yarn around the folded edge, exactly on track, and bring it through to the front again through the two layers of canvas along the edge of finished needlepoint.

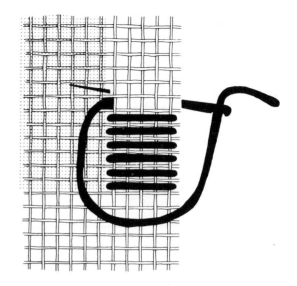

Brick

This may be the most versatile stitch pattern of all. It is fast, very easy to compensate, and useful at all times. It is the basic stitch of all Bargello designs, which are essentially just differently patterned versions of this Straight Gobelin stitch. As it covers four canvas threads, it is not always appropriate, especially where a large loopy stitch might become caught in buttons or buckles. But it lends itself easily to miniaturizing, and can be worked over two threads as well.

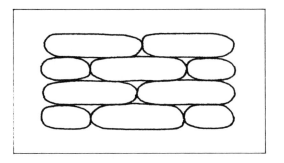

1. Emerge through the darkened hole at the lower left of the work to be covered. (As you can see here, the stitches will be horizontal; if you wish them to be vertical, simply turn your canvas sideways and begin to work.) Bring your yarn over four vertical canvas threads and emerge not in the next row up, but two canvas threads up.

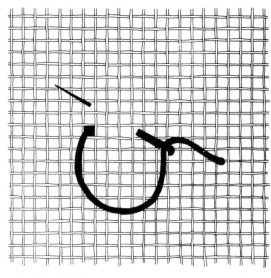

2. Again bring your yarn straight to the right over four vertical canvas threads and emerge two rows directly above your starting point. Your stitches will all line up evenly one above the other, with an empty row in between.

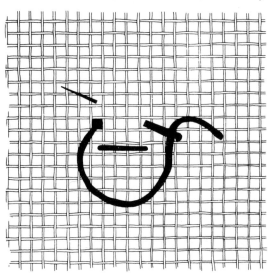

3. Continue in this manner.

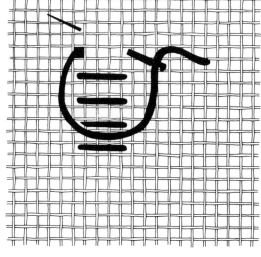

4. The next row is worked in the empty space above your first stitch. Emerge through the darkened hole that is situated two horizontal canvas threads in from your starting point. This stitch is called the Brick stitch because it is laid down like bricking, one stitch placed exactly midway above the other. Bring your yarn across four vertical threads and emerge in the empty row two rows up. Your far edge will always be jagged until you do your final compensating stitches. If your rows are lining up evenly, you are making a mistake.

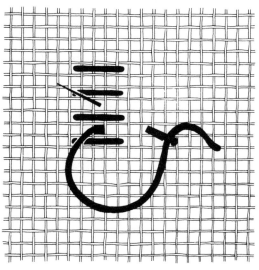

5. Here is an example of how you would compensate around an uneven design. Your far ends will always compensate with a simple one-, two-, or three-mesh stitch.

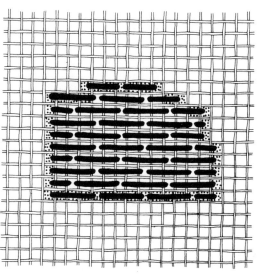

Byzantine

This stitch creates the illusion of motion. It works up quite quickly and is easily compensated at the end of each row with a single Tent stitch. However, it can be a bit difficult to count, as each stitch tends to obscure the canvas around it. Mistakes occur most often when the needlepointer inadvertently slants over one instead of two vertical canvas threads. As the yarn covers the canvas so well, it may then be hard to discover the initial mistake. When the Byzantine is worked around an intricate motif, it may also be difficult to keep in mind the rhythm of the stitch. But even if you do make an occasional mistake, only you will know it is there.

Like the Gobelin, of which this is a variation, the Byzantine can be worked over any number of canvas threads. It is limited only by the use to which you will put your work. If the finished piece is to receive a great deal of use or abuse, the tighter the stitch the better. The "steps" can also be made shorter or longer, or even asymmetrical.

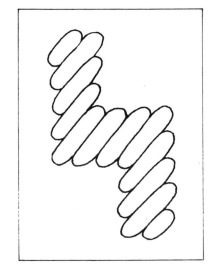

1. Start at the upper left of the area to be worked. This stitch must begin with a small compensating stitch. Bring your needle up through the darkened hole, and work a single slanted stitch up to the right. Emerge directly under the darkened hole.

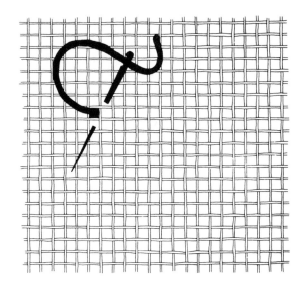

2. After the initial compensating stitch, slant your stitches up to the right across two vertical and two horizontal canvas threads. The needle emerges one hole beneath the previous stitch.

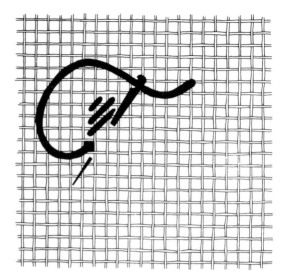

3. After you have worked nine fully formed stitches that move down your canvas, change direction and begin moving to the right with the same up-and-over-two stitch. Note that the last stitch in each direction serves as the first stitch in the changed direction, but your small compensating stitch does not count at all.

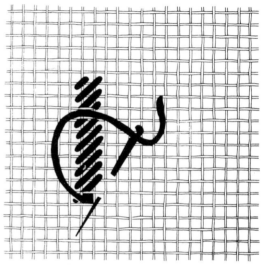

4. When you have worked nine stitches to the right, change direction again, and begin working your nine stitches down your canvas. Remember to count the last stitch of the previous row as the first stitch in this row.

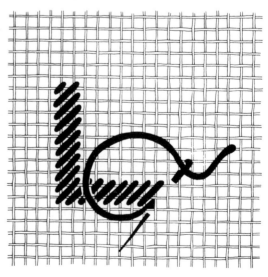

5. Continue stepping down until you have your nine stitches completed.

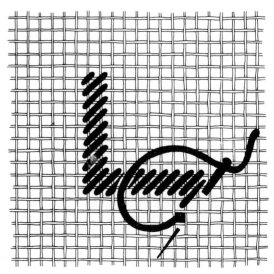

6. The second row starts just as the first did, with a small compensating stitch. Note that the first row has ended with a small compensating stitch as well. An interesting variation is to have a single row of the Continental stitch between each row of the larger Byzantine.

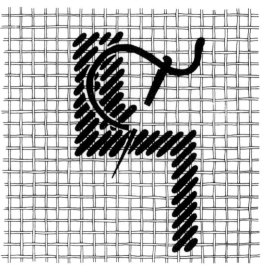

Continental

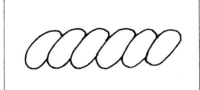

This is the most versatile, the most popular, and the most basic needlepoint stitch. One very good reason for its popularity is that it is easy to learn. Despite some disadvantages when compared to the Basketweave, it is nonetheless the most important stitch of all, and one that everyone who aspires to do needlepoint must know.

The Continental, the Basketweave, and the Half-Cross all look the same on the front of the canvas, but they are quite different on the reverse side, and this is important. The Half-Cross leaves most of the back of the canvas exposed, so it is not recommended at all. The Basketweave works with the weave of the canvas and therefore will not distort your piece. The Continental covers the back nicely, but its rows worked from right to left go against the warp and woof of the canvas so the work gets pulled badly out of shape. The Continental also requires that your work be turned at the end of each row—a dreadful nuisance. But the Continental does have one great advantage over the Basketweave, and that is that it can go anywhere; it can cover a tiny area of one or two stitches, and it can work lines only one stitch wide. The Basketweave cannot. Therefore, if you had the patience or the desire to learn only one stitch, it would have to be the Continental. Despite its disadvantages, it can do anything.

When a canvas is badly distorted, it can generally be blocked back into shape after the work is completed. But very large projects, such as rugs or wall hangings that are worked in one piece, are likely to become so distorted that it is impossible to get them back onto shape. Working the Basketweave wherever possible is one way to avoid this gross distortion. Another way is to use a frame, which slows you down a great deal because you cannot bring your needle forward to the front of the canvas with each stitch, but must pull it through to the back before coming forward again.

There is one more way to work the Continental without distorting your canvas, but it is extremely wasteful of yarn. I learned this method almost by accident. A customer came into my shop with a piece of work that was hardly distorted at all, yet she had worked it in the Continental. After studying the back for some time, I realized what she had done. She had worked each row, starting at the right, and when a row was completed, she simply wove her yarn under in back and snipped it off *instead of turning her canvas upside down and continuing back. Then she began again at the right with a new strand of yarn. In this way she never turned her canvas at all. Not only does this method waste a great deal of yarn, but, care must be taken to avoid ending all strands in the same place mid-row in each succeeding row or you will have a ridge. But doing the Continental this way does work. I have tried it myself, especially in places where I had a great deal of background and wanted to avoid the faint diagonal lines that may appear, willy-nilly, in large areas of Basketweave.*

My advice to the reader is to learn the Continental by all means. But also learn the Basketweave—the stitch of experts!

---

1. The Continental always begins in the upper right-hand corner of the area to be covered. Bring the needle up through the darkened hole, slant up and over one intersection of canvas threads, take your needle through to the back, and in the same motion emerge to the front of your canvas one hole to the left of the darkened hole.

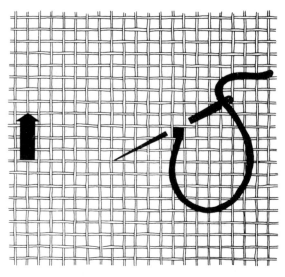

2. Continue working these small stitches, always slanting, always covering only one intersection, and always moving your row toward the left. The arrow indicates the top of your canvas. When it points down, it will mean that your work should be turned upside down.

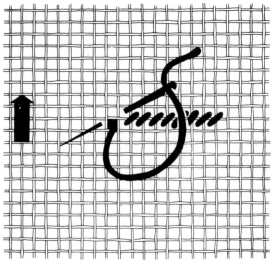

3. Individually, each little slanted stitch is sometimes called a Tent stitch, presumably because it slants up like the side of a tent. But when it is worked in a formation or in rows from right to left, it is called the Continental. The first row is completed when you have worked the final little Tent stitch and pulled your needle and yarn all the way through to the back instead of emerging to the front of your canvas. Now turn your canvas upside down.

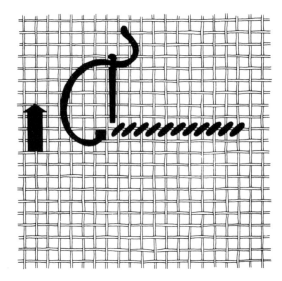

4. Begin the second row, once again working from right to left, by bringing the needle through the darkened hole, sharing that hole with a previous stitch. Work a Tent stitch as before, emerging one hole to the left. Each small Tent stitch will share a hole with the stitch in the previous row.

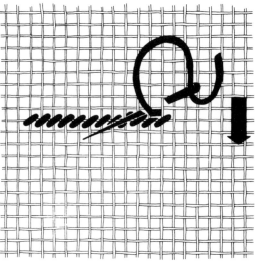

5. Continue across your row, moving toward the left one intersection at a time. When you reach the end of the row, pull your needle through to the back after working your last Tent stitch, and turn your canvas again so your work is now right side up.

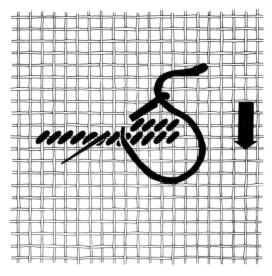

6. The Continental formation can also be worked from top to bottom. When you reach the bottom, turn your canvas upside down.

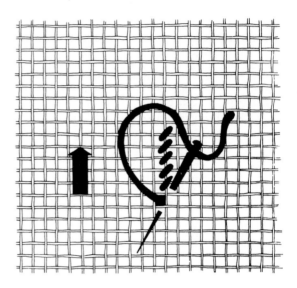

Cross-Box

This is a wonderful border stitch. It stands very high, frames your work beautifully, and looks especially effective in light colors. Colors can even be mixed within one box for a rainbow effect, but then your yarn must be anchored with knots at the back because this stitch leaves almost no back cover at all. It is not an easy stitch to compensate, but it can be done by skipping one hole. The yarn will hide this, and the eye will not usually discover that a few boxes are wider or narrower in one dimension. When using this stitch as a border around my work—as in the Geometric Sampler—if I am unsure that it will come out even, I start my border at the center top and work outward in both directions. As I near the corners, I count the canvas threads to see if my boxes will fit evenly. If not, I must compensate.

The boxes, unless you are compensating, always cover an uneven number of canvas threads—for example, five-by-five or nine-by-nine. Therefore, if I were working a five-thread box, I would start at the center top of my work. When I had reached a point about 3 inches from each corner I would stop and count my canvas threads. If, for instance, I found I had thirty-three remaining canvas threads to the corner, I would then decide to scatter three boxes six threads wide (they will still be five threads high) among three normal boxes of five threads wide, being sure to end with a five-thread box at the corner.

Repeat this procedure on each side. Find the approximate center and then work out toward the corners so you will not find yourself left with two or three canvas threads just at the corner, which would make for a box so distorted that it would surely be noticed.

Because the Cross-Box requires that you keep turning your canvas counterclockwise, it is recommended that on your raw mesh border you pencil in an arrow pointing to the top of your work. Be sure, as you work, that your arrow points in the same direction as that on the diagram you are following.

1. Bring the needle through the darkened hole, take it on a diagonal to the left, up and over five canvas threads, and emerge five horizontal threads straight down. Be sure your needle has emerged on a line with the darkened hole.

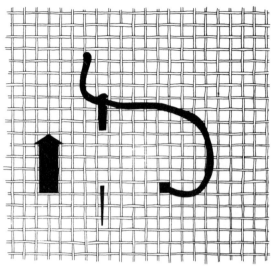

2. With the arrow still in the up position, complete the second arm of your X by crossing on a diagonal to the right, up and over five canvas threads again. Now, always remaining inside the X, take your needle straight to the left across the top of your X, and emerge in the farthest empty hole. Give your canvas one turn counterclockwise so your arrow runs beneath your X and points to the left.

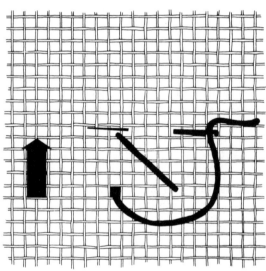

3. Now we begin a pattern that keeps repeating itself. Diagonal to the top of your X into the farthest empty hole, reach straight left across the back of your canvas along the top of your X, and emerge at the farthest empty hole. Give your canvas one turn counterclockwise.

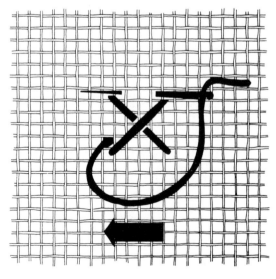

44

4. Your penciled arrow should now be on the right side of your X, pointing down. Repeat the instructions as previously outlined: diagonal to the top of your X into the farthest empty hole; reach straight across the top of your X to emerge in the farthest empty hole to the left; and, once again, give your canvas one turn counterclockwise.

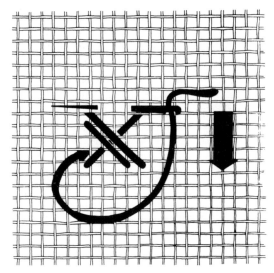

5. Note the direction of your arrow and repeat the previous instructions.

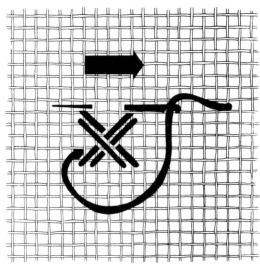

6. With the arrow now on the left and pointing upward, repeat.

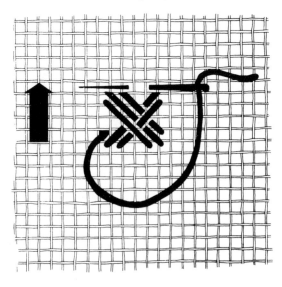

7. The arrow is now on the bottom and pointing left. As you proceed, it gets harder to see the empty holes. Be sure to push aside previous stitches so you don't accidentally skip a hole. This time when you diagonal right, up to the top into the farthest empty hole and reach across the top to the left, you will notice that *this* "farthest" hole is only one canvas thread away. Emerge through this hole and give your canvas one turn counterclockwise.

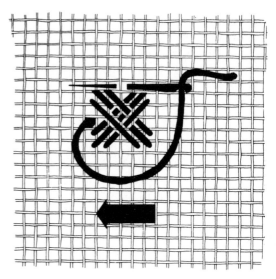

8. Repeat as before.

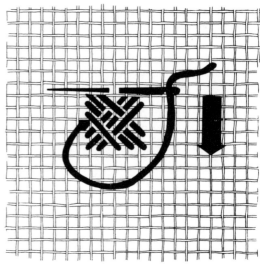

9. Repeat again.

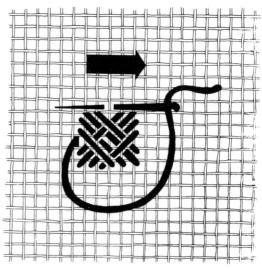

10. With your arrow on the left pointing upward, work your final stitch by crossing up to the last empty hole. Your Cross-Box is now complete. You probably will not have enough yarn left on your needle to start another box formation, so weave under the bit you have as best you can, through the little outline square of yarn that is on the back of your canvas. Start your next box by sharing a hole in the lower left-hand corner of this box (shown here shaded) or in the shaded hole shown to the right.

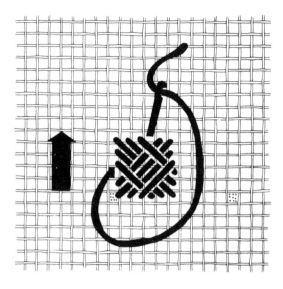

Diagonal Cross

This small stitch works up quickly and easily and is the basis for many lovely variations, two of which will be shown here. Several others will be treated separately, notably the Smyrna and its variations. The Diagonal Cross does not cover as well as the Upright Cross in Diagram 7, but it works up more quickly and forms a nice bumpy-textured surface. It also compensates more easily.

1. Begin near the upper right-hand side of your work, bringing your needle out through the darkened hole. Reach to the left across two vertical canvas threads and up and over two horizontals, and emerge straight down behind two horizontal canvas threads.

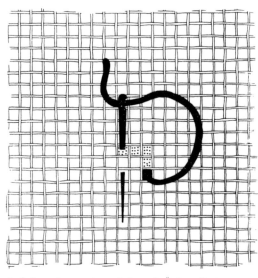

2. Complete the second arm of your X by reaching up and over two canvas threads to the right. Note what happens next because this is where most mistakes are made. Carefully emerge right back in the hole you have just vacated, taking care not to split the thread already there.

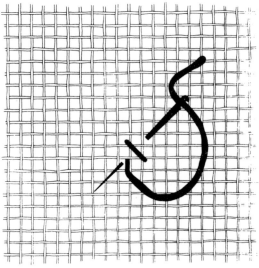

3. Repeat as before, moving up and over two canvas threads to the left for the first arm of another X. Continue this way. Your next row will begin two horizontal threads below your first row, again beginning on the right-hand side. If you wish, finish your final stitch of each row, and then turn your work upside down and head back again from right to left.

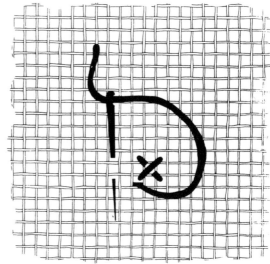

4. This diagram shows how easily the Diagonal Cross can be compensated if your piece has uneven borders. Be sure that the top stitch of your X *always* points up to the right.

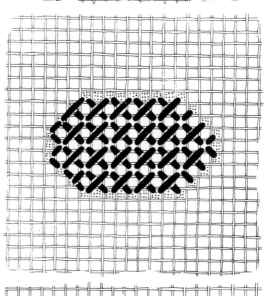

5. Here is the Upright Cross stitch. It is a wonderfully tight little stitch and gives a great textured look. But it is time-consuming to work, and can be a bit difficult to see if you are working on fairly fine canvas. Note that compensating is not difficult. To avoid making mistakes, be sure that the top part of your cross always runs horizontally. The stitch would lose its neat appearance if your top stitch varied from horizontal to vertical.

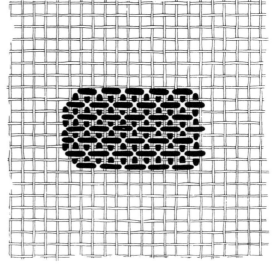

6. Here is another variation of the Cross stitch. The uncovered canvas is *left uncovered* to become part of the effect. I used this in my Rainbow Wallhanging sampler and I loved the look. If you would like to cover the canvas, however, you might fill the spaces with French Knots. There are many Cross stitches, but every one of them is a variation of the Upright and the Diagonal. Experiment with mixing and matching the two together and see what you can come up with. Remember that color plays an important part as well, and it can create an infinite number of possibilities.

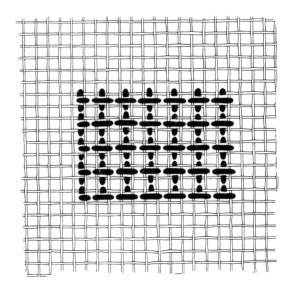

Diamond Eye

The Diamond Eye is a close relative of the Algerian Eye and, like it, is a pulled stitch. This means that the yarn is deliberately given a slight pull or tug after each stitch in an effort to distort the canvas to conform to your design. In this case we will open the eye in the middle of the stitch. Again I will use a painful figure of speech in an effort to help the reader avoid a common mistake that completely destroys the effect of the Diamond Eye formation. Be sure that the needle always goes into the eye. It never comes out of the eye.

One ply of Persian yarn is usually enough for any mesh, but it is worthwhile to experiment a bit. If your eye is not opening wide, you are probably using too heavy a yarn. Use a clean sponge to moisten the area to be worked so that it will pull more easily. I would advise against using this formation if too much compensation is required, although half or quarter formations of the stitch are not difficult.

1. Bring your needle out through the darkened hole, which will be the center top of your pattern, and then go straight down over four horizontal canvas threads into the shaded hole that will become the eye. In the same motion, reach up in back of the canvas to emerge one hole diagonally to the left and down from the darkened hole. Give a slight tug to your yarn to open the eye. Hold the tail of yarn taut with your other hand when you tug. The tail will be anchored by your following stitches.

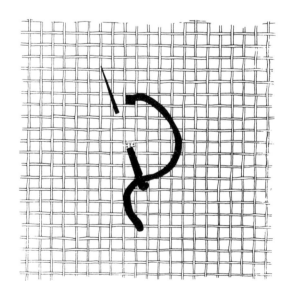

2. Again, put your needle into the eye and emerge one hole diagonally to the left of the darkened hole. Tug.

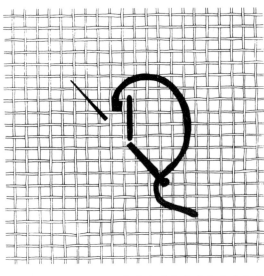

3. Repeat for two more stitches.

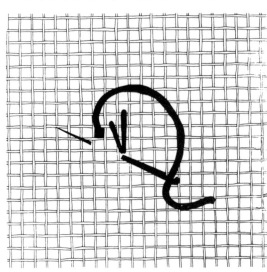

4. With this stitch you have reached one of the extreme points of your diamond. Now, after putting your needle into the eye, you will emerge one hole down diagonally to the *right* of the darkened hole. Move right and down toward the bottom point of your diamond. Tug.

5. Repeat until you have reached the bottom point, at which time your stitch will cover four horizontal canvas threads and will point straight up into the eye. After completing this stitch, emerge diagonally *up* and to the *right* one hole.

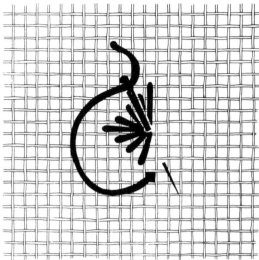

6. Continue to the extreme right-hand point, which you will have reached when you work a horizontal stitch covering four vertical canvas threads. Put your needle back into the eye, emerging diagonally up and to the *left* one hole.

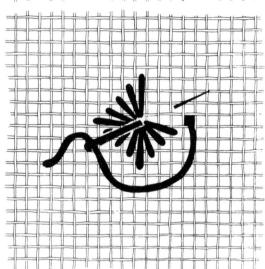

7. This diagram shows one Diamond Eye completed correctly. Note that the yarn tail is pulled upward away from the eye. In this way the eye is not obscured by yarn running behind it. If this one Diamond Eye motif is to stand alone, anchor your yarn in back, up and over the motif, to keep tension tight on the yarn. Diagram 8 of the Algerian Eye stitch (page 25) illustrates what you must *not* do. If you pull your yarn down behind the motif, the eye will close and you will have lost the effect entirely. Be sure if you are starting another Diamond Eye, that you pull the yarn up and away from the eye and begin the next motif from above.

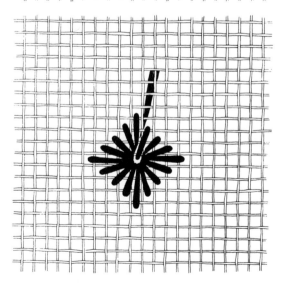

8. If you are planning a row of Diamond Eyes, the next one could begin as shown here. It might also begin either to the right of your completed motif or above it. If you wish to form another Diamond Eye beneath one already completed, start with a properly anchored fresh strand of yarn—do not use the same strand or you will distort the eye.

9. This diagram illustrates how you would compensate your Diamond Eyes. Turn to Diagram 10 of the Sheaf Stitch to see another variation that is quite lovely.

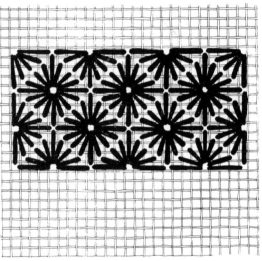

Double and Tie

This is an extraordinarily tight stitch, as it pads the canvas by doubling the threads in a single hole and then ties them down tightly. Therefore, it is one of the few decorative stitches that can be recommended unreservedly for rugs that will take a good deal of wear. Compensating is not difficult, but may reduce strength and durability.

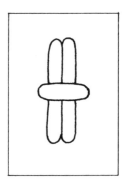

1. Bring your yarn out through the shaded hole and go straight up to cover four horizontal canvas threads. Emerge again through the shaded hole.

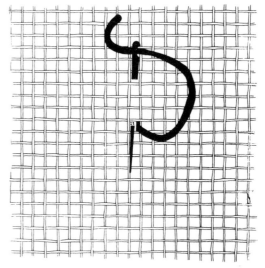

2. Again bring your needle up to repeat the first stitch in the very same holes to form a "twin" stitch, but this time emerge one space to the left and down two horizontal canvas threads.

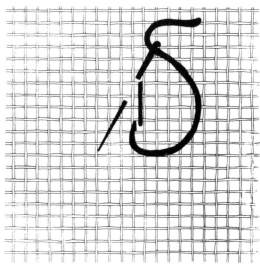

3. Tie your twin stitches down firmly by moving to the right over two vertical canvas threads. Emerge down under the darkened hole to the left, two horizontal canvas threads below the bottom of your upright stitches.

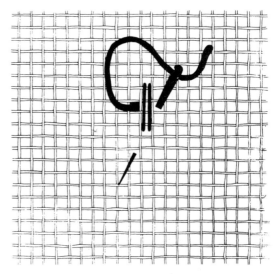

4. Start another set of twin stitches by reaching straight up and over four horizontal canvas threads, emerging in position to repeat the stitch.

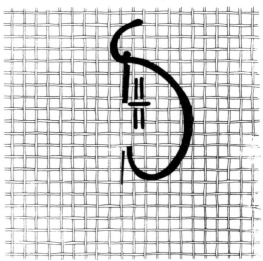

5. Complete your twin stitch and emerge one space to the left and down two horizontal canvas threads. This puts you in position to complete the stitch by tying it down across two vertical canvas threads to the right, emerging through the hole just vacated.

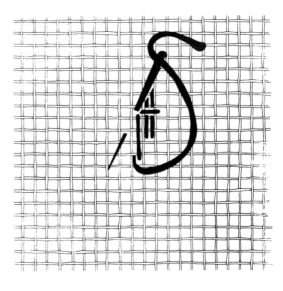

6. Your next stitch will begin by sharing a hole on the left side of your "tie" stitch. Then you will reach up and over four horizontal canvas threads to begin another pair of twin stitches. You will note that these Double and Tie formations are in a staggered position, one up, and one halfway down. This not only adds to the appearance of your work, but increases its strength and durability as well.

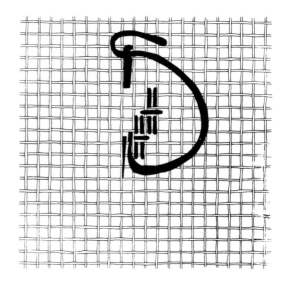

Feather

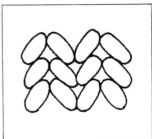

This stitch forms a true tent shape or teepee, and it is formed simply by placing a row of reverse Tent stitches beside regular Tent stitches. It is nice and tight, it is as quick as the Continental (of which it is a variation), but it gives a lovely effect. The feather is extremely easy to compensate because it covers only one intersection with each stitch.

1. Emerge through the darkened hole at the bottom right of your work, cross on a diagonal one canvas thread down to the right, and come through to the front just above your starting point.

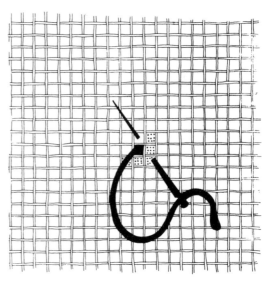

2. Continue upward in this manner.

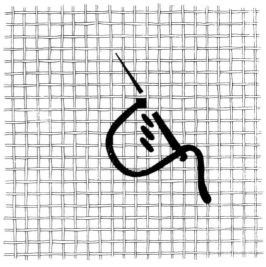

58

3. When you have reached the top of your row, start downward by working a Continental stitch that covers just one intersection of canvas threads up to the right to meet your topmost stitch. Emerge one hole down from your starting point, and continue down the row.

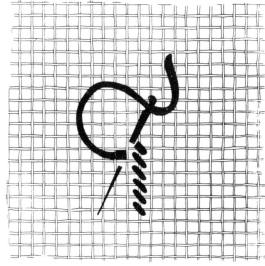

4. Begin a third row to match the first row. Each stitch should share a hole with a stitch from the previous row.

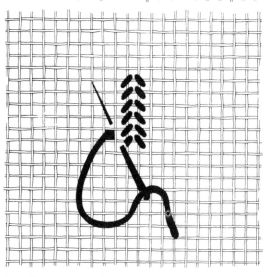

5. In working my Rainbow Wallhanging sampler, I soon became bored with all the stitches that I knew, so I began to invent variations. This is one of them. I simply enlarged the Feather by having it cover two intersections of canvas threads, and alternated it with the smaller version. Note the small compensating stitches used at the top and bottom of the enlarged form. For another variation, see Diagram 11 of the Smyrna Double-Cross stitch.

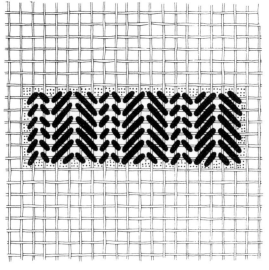

French Knot

This embroidery stitch has been borrowed for needlepoint. It forms a fat knot that sits on top of the canvas. It can be superimposed on canvas that has already been needle-pointed or, as shown here, worked on blank canvas. It makes a lovely center for flowers, curls for hair or lamb's wool, and is useful for a raised effect. There is no problem with compensation because a knot can be formed using the same hole for the emerging and exiting needle. Just be careful not to pull the finished knot through the hole! French Knots use up a great deal of yarn—a 23-inch strand of Persian yarn will work only about four knots.

---

1. Emerge where you wish to place your French Knot, shown here as the darkened hole. Hold your needle in a horizontal position above the canvas with your right hand, and, with your left, wind the yarn twice around the needle. Do not let go after winding.

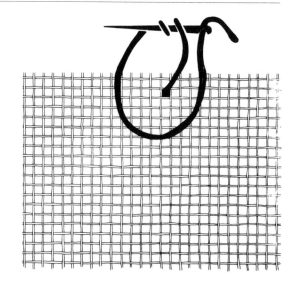

2. Now, still holding on with your left hand and keeping your windings tight, point your needle down through your canvas into any adjacent hole. As shown here, the needle is going into the hole diagonally up to the right. Push your needle through from the front of your canvas, and then reach behind to pull it all the way to the back. Allow the yarn to run loosely and smoothly through your left thumb and forefinger, which will guide it into a neat knot. Do not pull the yarn too tightly.

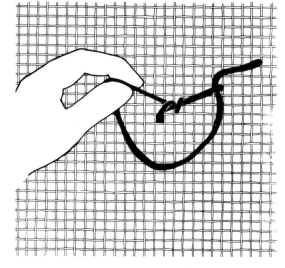

3. Here is a completed French Knot.

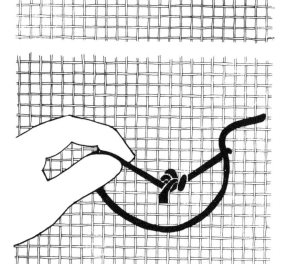

4. Your knots will not be too closely bunched if you begin as shown here, one mesh down from your former starting point, and again angle your knot one hole up to the right. Be sure to guide the yarn strand smoothly with your left thumb and forefinger as shown here.

5. Illustrated here are four completed knots as they might appear in a variation of the Irish Village Pillow on page 143.

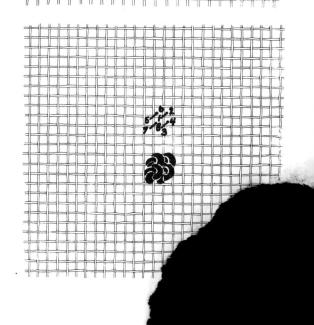

Gobelin

This is a rapid and useful stitch, and it can be worked over any number of canvas threads. The Gobelin can be worked straight, as in the Floral Fabric Pillow on page 121, or it can be worked slanted, as in the Decorative Panel and Skirt Border on pages 154 and 165. Although the slanted version will cover slightly better than the straight, both types cover a large amount of canvas quickly and well, and give a nice texture. Compensation is simple, with durability dependent only on the size of the stitch used.

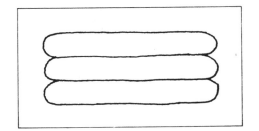

1. Bring your needle through the darkened hole, and across to the right over eight vertical canvas threads. Emerge one hole below your starting point.

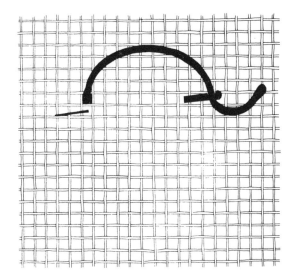

2. Continue in this manner, taking care that every stitch is the same length and perfectly straight in the proper position. The stitch demonstrated here covers eight canvas threads and forms quite a loopy stitch. If you need a tighter stitch, work over a smaller number of threads. Be consistent in each row.

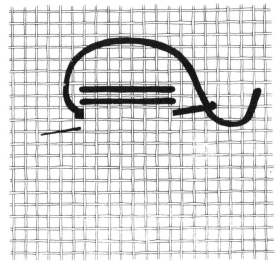

3. Here the straight Gobelin is shown covering only two vertical threads.

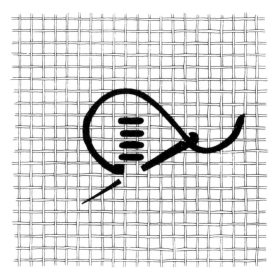

4. The slanted Gobelin shown here covers better, works up very quickly, but has a slightly different appearance. It is a bit harder to work because previous stitches are likely to obscure the hole you are seeking. It also compensates easily.

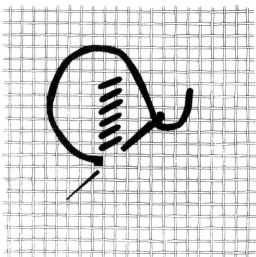

5. I used this variation to give the coat of my Harper's Lady a nice tweedy look (see page 113).

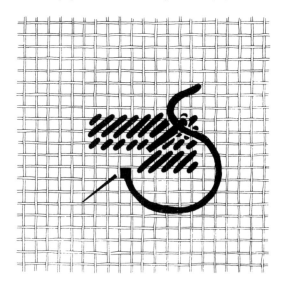

6. This is how the tweedy variation would compensate.

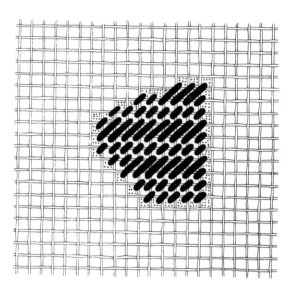

Greek

Everyone has favorite stitches, and this is one of mine. It works up very quickly, yet it gives a beautifully complex and textured feeling to your work. Mistakes are rare and easy to cover up. It is best used where you have a need for straight rows because it does not compensate especially well, but it does beautifully as several parallel rows of border or as filler in a large area. Its greatest drawback is that it does not cover the back of the canvas at all and, therefore, is not a long-wearing stitch.

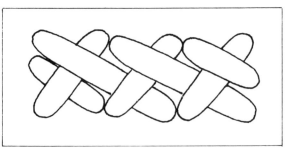

1. Start at the left side, one canvas thread down from your border. Bring the needle to the front through the darkened hole, and slant to the right across three vertical canvas threads, but down only two horizontals. Emerge three vertical canvas threads to the left, two holes down from the darkened one. This forms your starting compensating stitch.

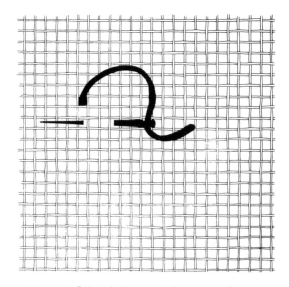

2. The Greek stitch now flows quickly and easily. Learn the rhythm; work up and to the right *over* three horizontal canvas threads, and then straight back and to the left *under* three vertical canvas threads.

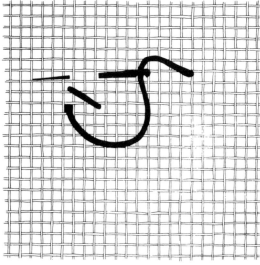

3. Now move down three and across six canvas threads, going straight back to the left *under* three threads.

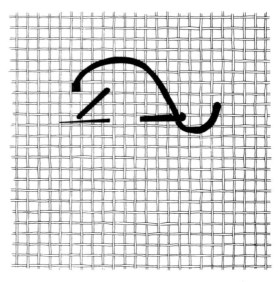

4. Once again, go up and to the right across three, and straight back to the left under three canvas threads.

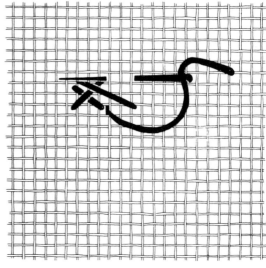

5. Again, go down three and across six, and straight back to the left under three canvas threads.

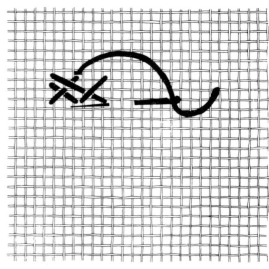

6. Once more, go up and to the right across three, and back to the left straight under three canvas threads. Continue in this way, forming a long stitch down to the right and then consolidating with a short stitch up to anchor it before commencing with another long stitch down. The Greek stitch has a lovely hypnotic rhythm that allows you to race along once you have caught onto it. Although not the most durable stitch, it will wear well if worked on a canvas 14 mesh or smaller.

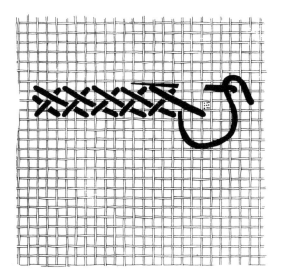

This diagram has a shaded hole to indicate how you would end the row. Form a final compensating stitch by pulling your needle to the back through the shaded hole. This final stitch ensures that there will not be a gap in your work with canvas showing at the end of a row. If you wish to turn the corner and work another row at right angles to the first, simply give your canvas a quarter turn counterclockwise, and begin another row as shown on Diagram 1, emerging through the blackened hole.

7. The Greek stitch can be worked over almost any number of stitches. Here it is shown worked over only two meshes.

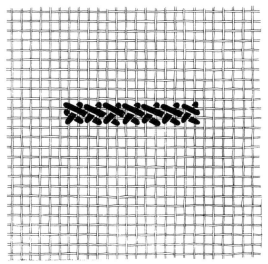

Knitting

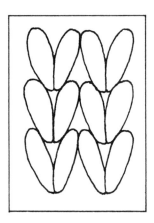

Quick and easy, this formation resembles the final look of a knitted piece. It forms rows and makes a nice textured filler, but it does not provide good cover for the back of the canvas and, therefore, should not be used extensively where durability is desired. The knitting stitch compensates very easily.

1. Start at the bottom right, one canvas thread in from your border. Bring the needle up through the darkened hole. Form a **V** by reaching over to the right one canvas thread and up two. Emerge again two threads straight to the left.

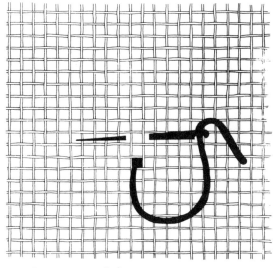

2. Reach back down to the right, sharing a hole at the point of the **V**, and emerge again two canvas threads directly to the left.

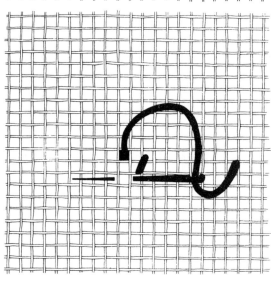

3. Reach up to the right to share a hole, and emerge two threads straight to the left. Continue in this manner, moving to the left, forming small V's.

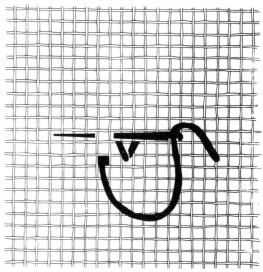

4. For the second row, bring the needle out two canvas threads above the *point* of the V; again reach to the right, up two and over one, emerging two canvas threads directly to the left.

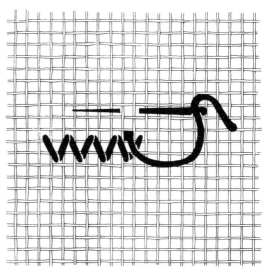

5. Continue to form V's, sharing a hole at the base and left arm of each previous V.

6. Where compensation is necessary, work the arms of the V up and over only one canvas thread.

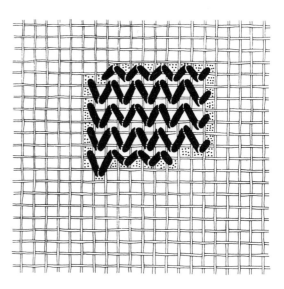

Leaf

This is a specialized stitch that really does resemble a leaf and, therefore, is useful wherever that type of look is appropriate. It will compensate, but not without a struggle.

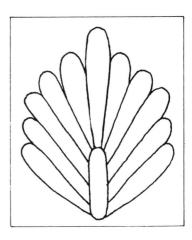

1. Start near the upper right-hand corner of your work, three canvas threads in from the right side border and eight canvas threads down from the top. Bring your needle through the darkened hole, cross on a diagonal up and over three canvas threads to the right, and emerge just above your starting point. Work another diagonal the same size just over this first stitch, emerging again directly above your starting point. Now work a third diagonal stitch (again the same length) above the first two, but this time emerge in the same hole that you have just vacated as shown in Diagram 2.

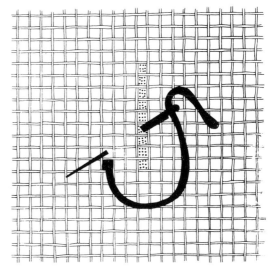

2. Now your pattern changes somewhat. From the hole you are sharing with the previous stitch (shown here as the darkened hole), reach up to the right, but this time you will be moving up *four* canvas threads and over only two. Emerge one hole directly above the darkened hole.

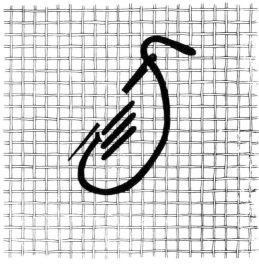

3. Again reach to cover four canvas threads up, but only *one* over to the right. Emerge through the hole just vacated.

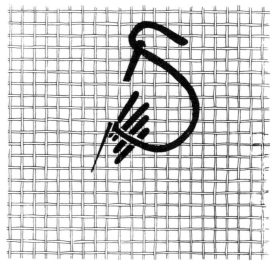

4. From the shared hole, this time reach straight up to the top of the leaf, and cover *five* horizontal canvas threads, emerging as before in the hole just vacated.

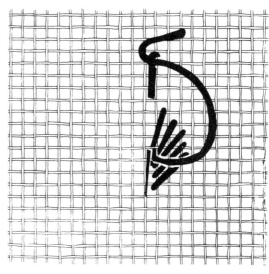

5. Now it is time to work down the other side of your leaf. Simply reverse the pattern used on the previous side. Note that your first stitch on the left side reaches up four canvas threads but over only one to the left before the needle again emerges through that just-vacated, much-used hole.

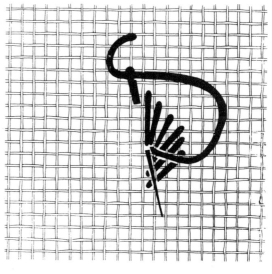

6. This diagram shows your leaf almost complete. It might be helpful to note that the third and fourth stitches share the same hole as the eighth and ninth. The fifth, sixth and seventh stitches share a common hole, while the second and tenth share a hole, and the first and eleventh do likewise. As you complete your leaf, check to be sure that each stitch on the left side lines up evenly with its counterpart on the right. You should be able to spot a mistake fairly quickly, as the finished leaf should be quite uniform on both sides.

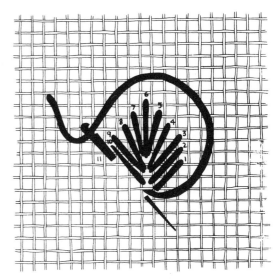

7. This final stitch provides a stem of sorts. Move straight up over three canvas threads, which are difficult to count because they are now hidden by your previous stitches. But you will note the needle is going once again into that most heavily filled hole that was the starting point of your three topmost stitches. Your needle now emerges through the shaded hole that is on a line with the bottom of your leaf, six vertical canvas threads to the left of it.

8. The first stitch of your new leaf will, as before, cross on a diagonal up and over to the right to cover three canvas threads. This time the tip end of your first stitch will share a hole with a previous stitch. Your second and third similar diagonal stitches will also share holes with the previous leaf, but the three topmost stitches will not.

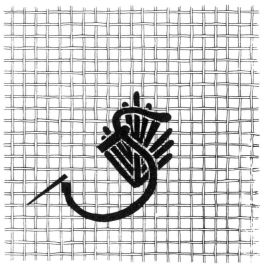

9. This diagram illustrates several compensation possibilities.

74

Milanese

This is a very decorative and pretty stitch, but for some reason it is a bit confusing to a few people, including me. If each succeeding row is worked in a different color, it is exceptionally beautiful. Each row fits as neatly as one jigsaw-puzzle piece into the next. It is really an abbreviated form of the Scotch stitch, but it looks very different. Compensating is possible, but it does tend to increase the confusion quotient.

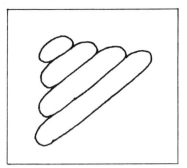

1. The Milanese moves on a diagonal path from the upper left-hand corner of your work to the lower right. Bring your needle through the darkened hole, cross on a diagonal up and over one intersection of canvas threads, to the right and emerge directly below your starting point. This little stitch sets the top and left borders of this individual motif. Each succeeding stitch will line up with the first along the top and left sides.

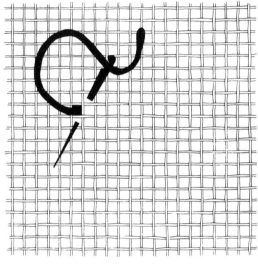

2. Cross on a diagonal up to the right over two intersections of canvas threads. Emerge again directly below your starting point.

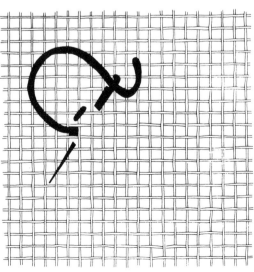

3. Reach up and over to the next empty hole in the top, emerging back down at the left side in the empty hole beneath the darkened hole.

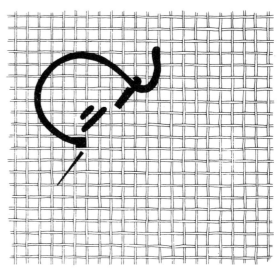

4. Reach up and over to the right to the top again, thus completing this individual motif composed of four parallel expanding stitches. You must now emerge in position to start your next individual motif. Here is where some of the confusion arises, so it is important to learn this correctly. I have found it best *not* to trust the eye, but to *count* carefully down three horizontal canvas threads from your needle's exit at the top, and then two vertical canvas threads to the left. This is shown in the diagram as a shaded path of holes. *Down three and left two* is the secret password.

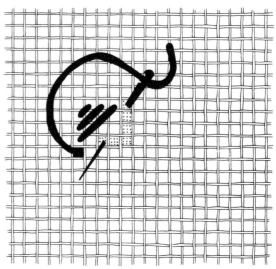

5. Begin with your smallest stitch covering just one intersection, which again sets your topmost and leftmost borders, and work your individual motif of four parallel expanding stitches. Then once again reach down three and left two to begin the next. Continue in this manner.

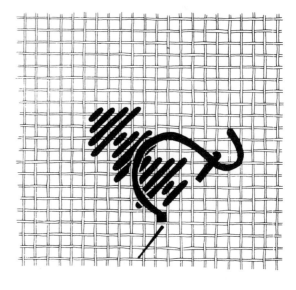

6. Your return trip may also be a bit confusing, but it need not be if you remember certain helpful hints. Your smallest stitch should *always* nestle against and share a hole with the largest stitch of your previous row. This is a great help, because on the way *up* you get into position to start a new motif by reaching *three canvas threads to the left and two down*, instead of vice versa as before. But this is made much easier by the knowledge that the smallest stitch always shares a hole with the largest stitch of the previous row, so you may not even have to count after the first row.

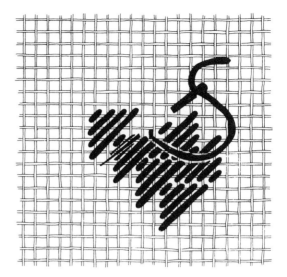

7. Compensating stitches are easy to form because they cross up to the right only as far as the border permits. What *is* difficult, is keeping the pattern firmly enough in mind throughout the distortions caused by working around another design.

As a further memory aid, look again at Diagram 4 and note that it is also possible to locate the new starting point by counting two canvas threads to the right and one up from the *bottom* of the final stitch. This also puts you in a position to begin a new Milanese four-stitch motif, and would prove especially helpful in the event that the topmost point had to be abbreviated and therefore could not serve as a counting aid.

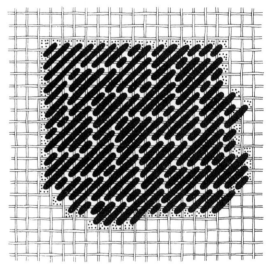

Parisian

This is a lovely, quick, and useful stitch. Worked by itself in many colors, it can form a kaleidoscopic design that is fun to work and not hard to manage. Compensating is not too difficult, and because the Parisian is primarily made up of small stitches, it will fit most designs well and will take a good deal of abuse.

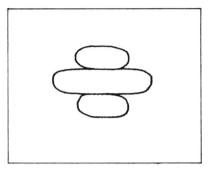

1. Starting at the lower left, emerge through the darkened hole and bring your yarn over four vertical canvas threads. Come through to the front again on the next row up, one hole in from the left-hand border.

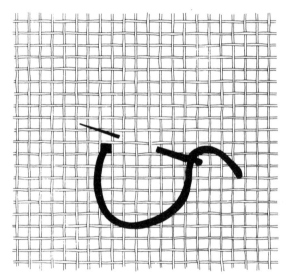

2. Bring the yarn across to the right over just two vertical canvas threads, emerging one row above on the far left-hand border. Form a large four-canvas-thread stitch and continue in this manner, alternating large four-canvas-thread stitches with small two-canvas-thread stitches. Your stitches should be forming a jagged edge on both sides.

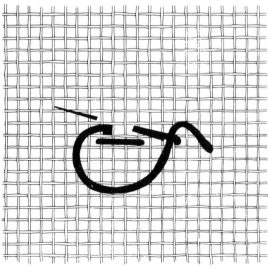

3. The second row begins with a small two-canvas-thread stitch, then a four-canvas-thread stitch, and so on. Your edges will always be jagged until you compensate.

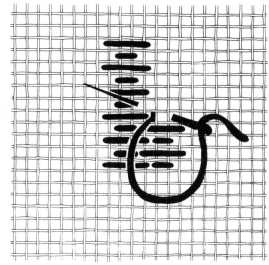

4. Here is an example of how this stitch might compensate if it had one uneven border.

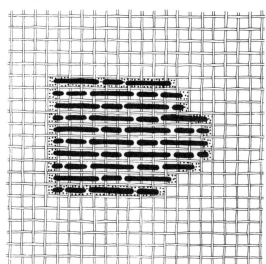

5. This is a diagonal variation of the Parisian stitch. It forms the same small, large, small pattern, but the stitches are formed by diagonals instead of straight stitches. It is also very similar to the Scotch stitch. Start in the upper left-hand corner of your work. Bring your needle through to the front of your canvas one hole under the corner hole. Work a small Tent stitch up and over to the right across one mesh. Emerge immediately below, and work a larger diagonal stitch up to the right over two meshes. Emerge immediately to the right of where you came out previously, and work another small Tent stitch up to the right over just one mesh. Reach straight down the canvas behind two horizontal canvas threads to be ready to start your next stitch pattern. Repeat as before, working your way down the canvas in a diagonal line. The second row starts in the first empty hole on the upper left-hand side of your work.

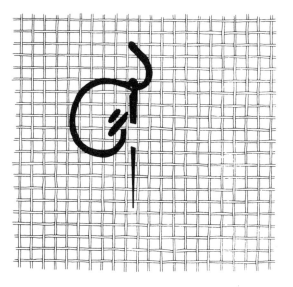

6. This diagram shows how you might compensate and how each little Mosaic variation fits into the next.

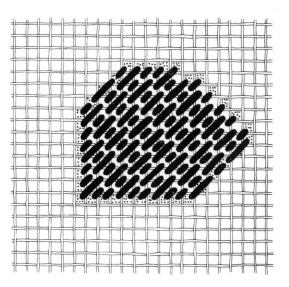

Pulled-Thread

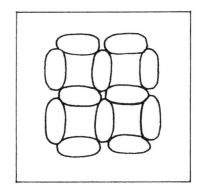

This is one of a group of stitches that gets pulled in order to deliberately distort the canvas, pulling it out of shape to create a certain effect. The Algerian Eye and Diamond Eye stitches are also pulled, but they are not nearly as lacy or as open. This stitch is a great favorite of mine. I used it for the hat of the Harper's Lady (page 113) to achieve the effect of loosely woven straw, and I used it frequently in my Rainbow Wallhanging sampler (page 141) in appreciation of its light, open effect. It is not a durable stitch, but it sure does get a lot of comment! I use a single ply of yarn and work each stitch twice to maximize the pull. It helps also if you take a small clean sponge and wet just the area of canvas that you will be working; it will then distort more easily. Many people like to use a small frame—either the roll type or a hoop—to maintain an even pressure. It is not absolutely necessary, but it does help to give your work a smooth and uniform look. Compensation is possible and not too difficult, but too much will spoil the geometric effect.

1. Firm tension on your yarn is important, so it is best to tie a good-sized knot at the end of your strand. Pull the yarn through to the back of the canvas some distance from where you will start. Leave the knot protruding on the *front* of your canvas. It will be cut off later, but it is helpful now to hold the yarn taut. Bring your needle up through the darkened hole, two canvas threads to the left of your top right-hand border. Cross two vertical threads to the right, and emerge through the hold just vacated. Give a good tug on your yarn to pull the canvas threads together.

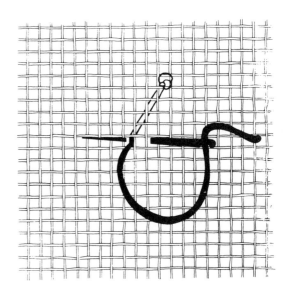

2. Move again across the same two vertical canvas threads to the right, and now diagonal down two horizontal canvas threads to the left, emerging in the second hole under your starting point. Tug.

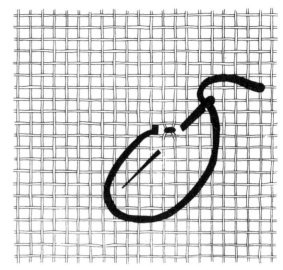

3. Now go straight up two horizontal canvas threads and emerge in the just-vacated hole, prepared to repeat this stitch. Tug.

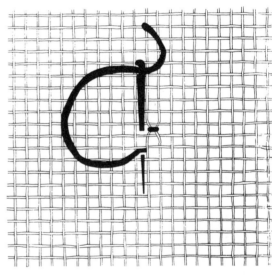

4. Repeat the previous stitch, but emerge diagonally down to the left two canvas threads from the darkened hole but in the same track. Tug.

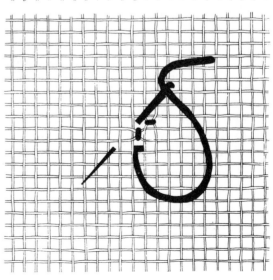

5. Cross over two canvas threads to the right. Note that you are forming steps going down to the left. Tug and repeat the previous stitch, this time emerging two canvas threads down to the left. Tug.

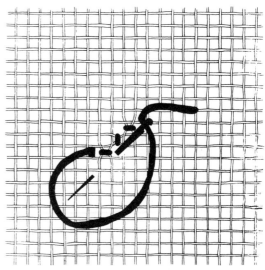

6. Again work two upright stitches, one on top of the other, across two canvas threads, with a sharp pull after each. This diagram shows only the first upright stitch being worked. After the second upright stitch, emerge diagonally two threads to the left. When you have finished one row it is best to stop. Weave your leftover yarn through the back, but be careful not to obscure any of the opened holes. Always maintain the tension on your yarn by weaving in the direction from which your last stitches originated. For example, if your last stitch came from the bottom moving upward, weave your leftover yarn carefully to the bottom, avoiding any opened holes. If you have finished needlepoint below your Pulled-Thread stitches, you may weave your leftover yarn through the back of this needlepoint in a downward motion to maintain your tension. If you have only raw canvas below your stitches, you may pull the yarn remaining on your needle forward to the front of the raw canvas, place it flat, and work your subsequent needlepoint stitches over it to anchor it firmly in place so that once again tension is maintained.

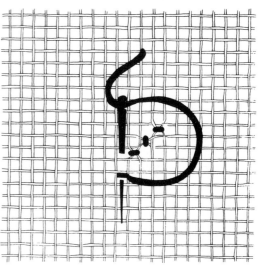

7. Begin your next row at the top, as you did for the first row. Once again leave a knot protruding somewhere on the front of your canvas where it will remain until you are sure that the tension will hold; then cut it off and pull the tail through to the back to be woven under and snipped off. If you are starting to the right of your previous row, your first stitch will be a small upright over two canvas threads, sharing a hole. Tug and repeat, emerging diagonally to the left to share a hole with the second and third stitches of your first row (shown here shaded).

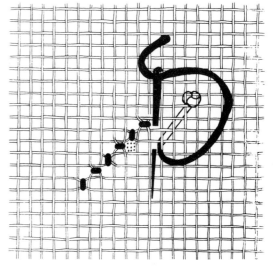

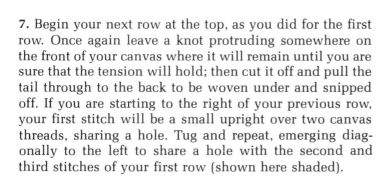

8. All rows to the *left* of the first row will start with a small stitch moving from left to right over two canvas threads. This diagram shows a row to the left in progress.

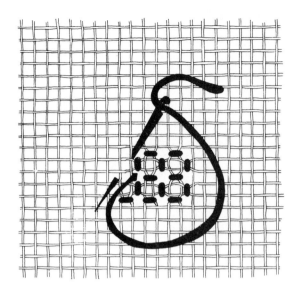

Rice

This is another type of interesting Cross stitch. It lends itself well to the use of many colors. The initial large **X** may be worked in one color and the little ties across the arms worked in another to create a very lovely effect. My diagrams generally show the fastest and easiest way to work each stitch in one color, but this will not, I hope, discourage you from experimenting with other effects. This stitch covers well and looks extremely complex on the canvas, although it is really very simple to do. Compensating is not too difficult. On a 12 mesh or smaller canvas, the stitch is quite durable.

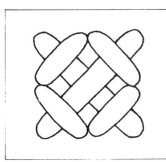

1. Start four horizontal canvas threads down from the upper right-hand corner of the area to be worked. Pull your yarn to the front through the darkened hole, cross diagonally to the left up and over four canvas threads, and emerge straight down four canvas threads. Check to be sure you are emerging on an even line with the darkened hole.

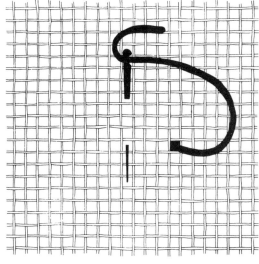

2. Complete the second arm of the **X** by crossing diagonally up and over four canvas threads to the right—making sure this arm is the same length as the first—and now emerge two vertical canvas threads directly to the left across the top of your **X**.

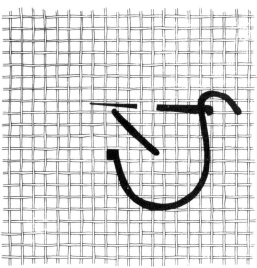

3. You are now going to tie down each arm. Cross on a diagonal down to the right over two canvas threads to the hole midway between the arms and emerge directly to the left, now in the center hole between the two arms on the left.

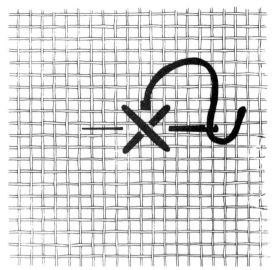

4. Now cross on a diagonal to the right, up and over two canvas threads into the already occupied hole that is midway between the arms at the top. Reach straight down to emerge again in the center hole on the bottom of the X.

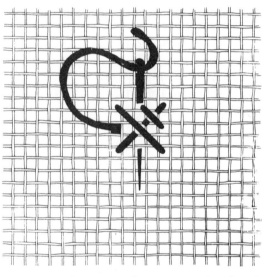

5. Diagonal up to the right to share a hole with your first little tie stitch, and then reach directly to the left to share a hole again in that hole midway between the arms on the left.

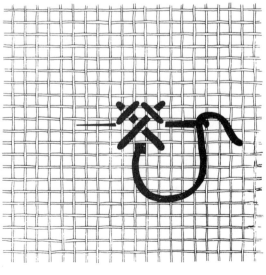

86

6. Diagonal down to the right to share a hole midway between the bottom arms to complete your final tie, and now emerge two canvas threads directly to the lower left-hand corner of your X to begin another Rice motif.

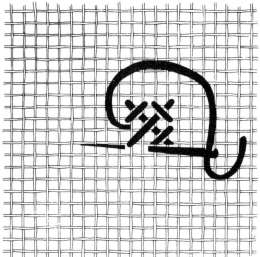

7. Repeat as before.

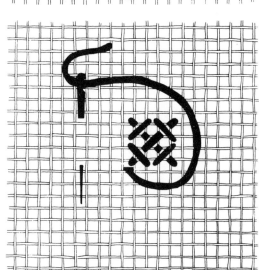

8. Your second row can sit right under your first.

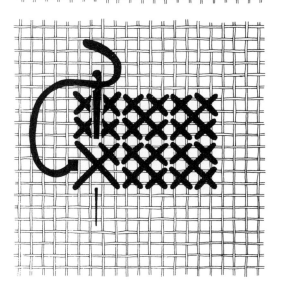

9. Note in this diagram that compensating stitches in general form small X's and are, therefore, hardly noticeable. In fact, you must study the diagram a bit to discover them.

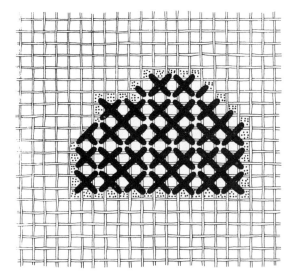

10. I worked out this variation for my Rainbow Wallhanging sampler. It proved very effective, I think. Note that the ties in this variation are smaller, and do *not* reach to the center hole between the arms of the X. They cover only one intersection of canvas threads and, in fact, leave the center hole empty for the French Knot. I call this variety of Rice stitch the Dumbbell stitch because each arm with its small tie resembles a dumbbell. Instead of a French Knot between each X, you might use a small two-canvas-thread Upright Cross stitch. In this way, if you were playing with color, you could work the large X in one color, the ties in another, and the small upright crosses alternating in two more colors.

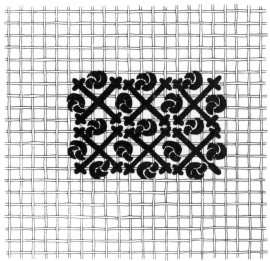

Scotch

This is a must stitch—versatile, effective, durable, quick to work, and easy to compensate. What more can one ask? It forms neat little boxes that are nicely delineated, and it lies flat so it is most effective when juxtaposed beside a textured or raised stitch such as the Smyrna Double-Cross.

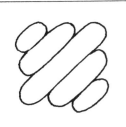

1. Begin one canvas thread down from the upper left-hand corner of the area to be worked. (The Scotch stitch can be worked in straight rows across if you prefer or if your design demands it, but it is faster and wastes less yarn if worked in diagonal rows. Once you get the rhythm of the stitch, it will not be too difficult to make it move whichever way you wish.) Pull your yarn to the front through the darkened hole, and cross on a diagonal up to the right over one small intersection of canvas threads. Emerge immediately below the darkened hole.

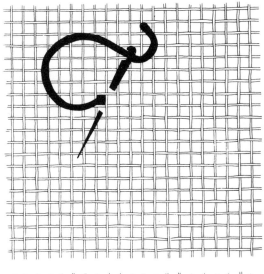

2. Angle up to the right again, this time covering *two* intersections of canvas threads. Emerge immediately below the darkened hole.

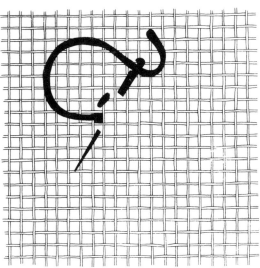

3. Repeat with a still larger stitch, covering three intersections of canvas threads, but now emerge immediately to the right of the darkened hole.

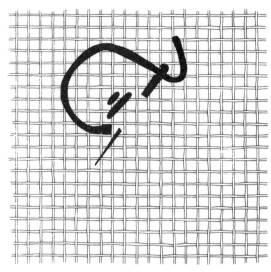

4. Your stitches have been expanding in size, but now they are contracting. Angle up to the right over only two intersections of canvas threads—just under the far tip of your previous stitch. Do not reach beyond your previous stitch. Emerge again immediately to the right of the darkened hole. Be careful here. You must not emerge *below* the darkened hole, but on a line even with it.

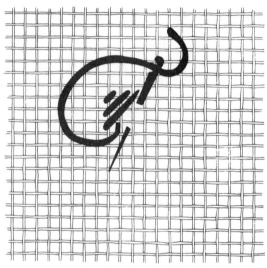

5. Angle up to the right over only one intersection of canvas threads and emerge straight down from behind two horizontal canvas threads. Do be sure that your needle is pointing down perfectly straight and not angling off somewhere to the left.

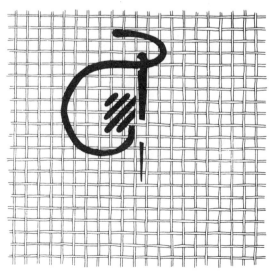

6. Your next motif begins by angling up to the right over one intersection of canvas threads. Emerge immediately below your starting point. Then repeat as before, expanding your slanting stitches to cover two and then three intersections of canvas threads before contracting your stitches again in reverse order. After the final small stitch of each motif, be sure to reach straight down two horizontal canvas threads to bring yourself into position to start the next motif.

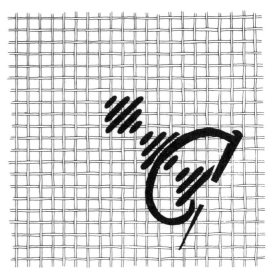

7. Your second row will nestle up against the first. This diagram shows where you will begin if you move to the right.

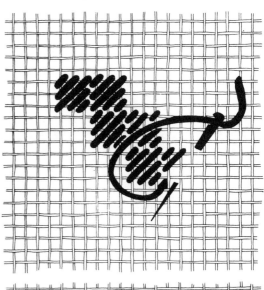

8. If you wish to start another row to the left of your first, go to the front in the first empty hole on the left-hand border and work your first small slanted stitch.

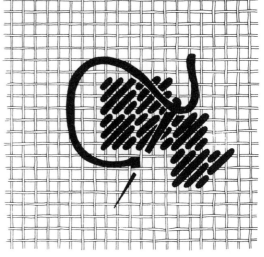

9. The Scotch stitch is quite easy to compensate. If your slanted stitches cannot cover the proper number of intersections, let them contract to cover what they can. Keep in mind the rhythm of this formation. If a stitch ought to slant up to cover two intersections of canvas threads, but due to a barrier of some kind it can only cover one, then it will have to cover just one. It can never cover *more* than it should. This holds true for all compensating stitches, which in general should be abbreviated but not expanded.

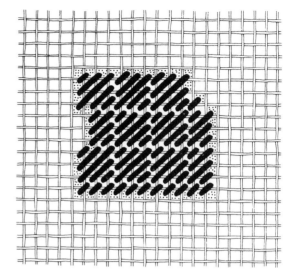

10. When alternate Scotch motifs reverse direction, the formation is called the Flat stitch. It is very effective, and takes on the form of diamonds within diamonds. When these are worked in different colors, as in the Geometric Sampler on page 147, it gives a beautiful effect. Try working all your smallest stitches (those covering only one intersection of canvas threads) in a very pale color, then work your two-canvas-intersection stitches with a slightly darker color, and with the darkest color, work your three-canvas-intersection stitches.

Sheaf

This stitch is almost too decorative to be used as a filler, but it can stand beautifully on its own. It covers the canvas very well, but it is difficult to compensate because it loses its appeal if pulled out of shape too much.

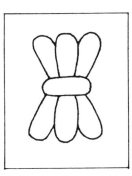

1. Begin four canvas threads down from the upper right-hand corner of the area to be worked. Pull your yarn through the darkened hole, reach straight up over four horizontal canvas threads, and emerge to the left of the darkened hole.

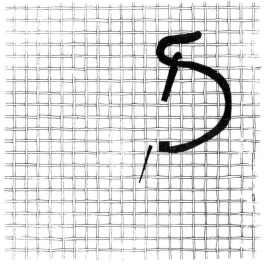

2. Again reach straight up and over four horizontal canvas threads, emerging to the left of the darkened hole. Be sure stitches are the same size.

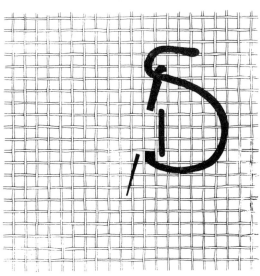

3. Once more, reach straight up and over four horizontal canvas threads, but this time emerge down two horizontal canvas threads *in the same track.* Be sure the needle is *outside* the loop of yarn remaining on your needle. You may have to hold your yarn to the right so your needle can pass to the left of the loop as shown here.

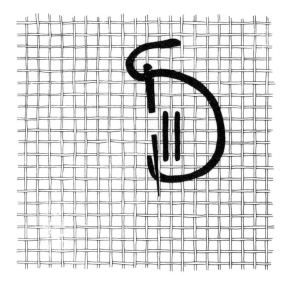

4. Now cross straight to your right only two canvas threads to form a little nip at the waist of your stitches. Then emerge in a shared hole at the lower left-hand corner of this Sheaf stitch, in position to begin another.

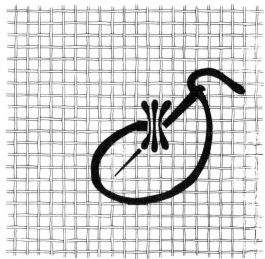

5. Repeat as before, starting with your first upright four-canvas-thread stitch.

6. Continue across the row, carefully pushing aside each third upright to find the center hole in the same track, and then nipping the waist with a two-canvas-thread stitch only.

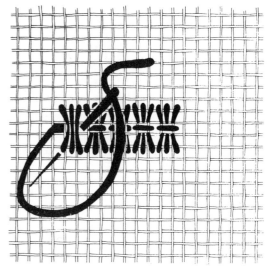

7. The second row starts beneath the first.

8. Your Sheaf stitch can be any size, larger or smaller. Note that in this upright form, the nip at the waist always covers one less canvas thread than there are uprights in the sheaf. Therefore, in the diagrammed variation shown here, in which there are two upright stitches, the nip at the waist covers just one canvas thread.

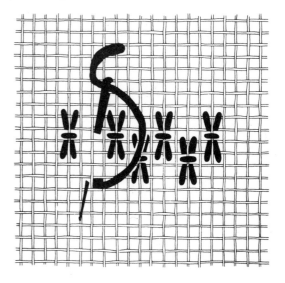

9. Here is a sloping variation that is quite beautiful and extremely decorative. The uprights cover first two, then four, then six, then eight horizontal canvas threads before contracting again in the reverse order. This form of the Sheaf gets a narrower waist. To work the tie, you must reach one canvas thread in under the Sheaf to share a track with the four-canvas-thread uprights. Emerge to share a hole with the bottom of the two-canvas-thread stitch on the left.

10. Here is a beautiful combination that I discovered while working my Rainbow Wallhanging sampler. I worked one row of sloping Sheaf stitches, with each motif separated by two vertical canvas threads. I filled these gaps with three uprights, covering two, then four, then two horizontal canvas threads. The next row was worked in a variation of the Diamond Eye. Necessity forced me to shorten its two vertical spokes. Another fine variation is illustrated in Diagram 9 of the Smyrna Double-Cross stitch. Take special note of the compensation on the right side.

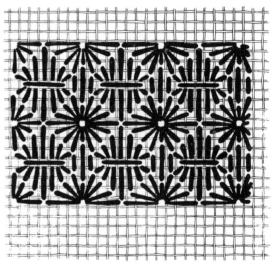

Smyrna Double-Cross

This little "bump" stitch is another of my favorites. It is fun to work, quick, and easy to do. It is very effective either in a single color or many, has any number of variations, covers well, and is easy to compensate. Basically it consists of a little two-canvas-thread diagonal cross perched on top of a larger four-canvas-thread upright cross.

1. Begin four canvas threads down and two in from the upper right-hand corner of the area to be worked. Bring your yarn to the front through the darkened hole. Reach straight up over four horizontal canvas threads and slant to the left to emerge from under two intersections of canvas threads.

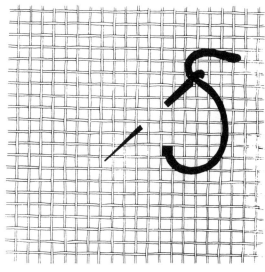

2. Complete the second arm of your upright cross by reaching straight across to your right over four vertical canvas threads. Emerge one intersection of canvas threads diagonally to the right and up from your darkened hole.

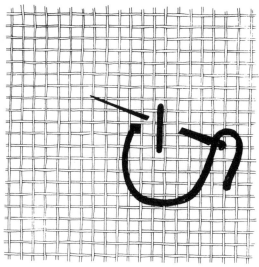

3. Cross on a diagonal down to the right across two intersections of canvas threads. Emerge straight left from behind two vertical canvas threads.

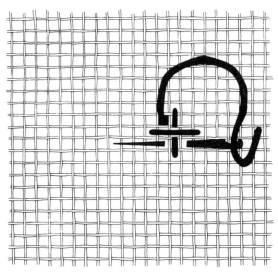

4. Complete the second arm of your little X by reaching up to the right over two intersections of canvas threads. Emerge four vertical canvas threads to the left of, and on an even line with, the bottom of your first motif, in position to begin another Smyrna Double-Cross. Repeat as before. (Note that the arms of the small diagonal cross form a nice slanted line with those of the upright cross. This should help you find the correct holes when working your topmost little diagonal cross.)

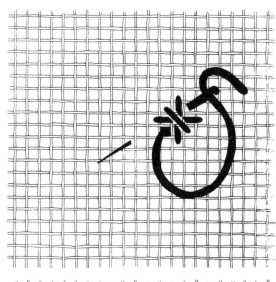

5. The second row goes under the first and fits neatly within it. Notice that the long upright arms touch the long horizontal arms of the adjacent row, and the small diagonal crosses share holes.

6. This diagram illustrates how you might find yourself compensating. If you are working your motifs correctly, the topmost stitch of each diagonal cross will always slant up to the right and never to the left. Be sure that this is what you are doing, as all your motifs must be uniform.

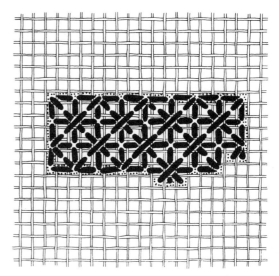

7. In this variation, a four-canvas-thread diagonal cross is worked first, and a four-thread upright cross sits on top. In this case, be sure that your topmost stitch is always horizontal. Note compensation.

8. This is a lovely variation. A four-canvas-thread diagonal cross has a two-thread upright cross on top. The spaces in between each motif are filled by another two-thread upright cross. Try working all the large X's in one color, alternate the small superimposed crosses with two more colors, and use a fourth for the filler crosses. Note the examples of compensation.

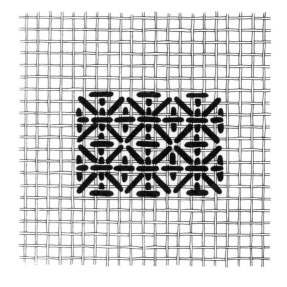

9. Here the Smyrna Double-Cross alternates rows with the sloping Sheaf stitch (see Diagram 9 of the Sheaf stitch) to create an unusual effect.

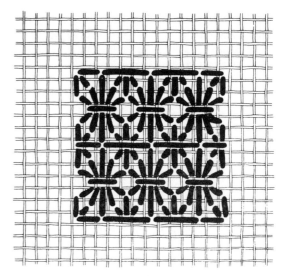

10. This diagram shows an interesting combination of the Feather and Smyrna Double-Cross with compensation.

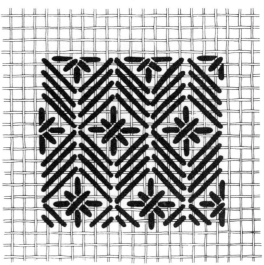

Turkey Knot

This stitch is used to create the illusion of fur, hair, or fringe. It can be left looped to resemble curls or fringe, or cut to give the shaggy appearance of fur or grass. It is versatile and easy, but time-consuming, and the loops use up a great deal of yarn. Compensating is no problem at all and is totally invisible.

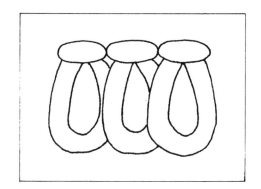

1. The Turkey Knot can be worked from the right or from the left, but it is always best to work from bottom to top. For the purposes of these diagrams, begin one hole in from the left border of the area to be worked. Pull your needle through to the back in one hole and out the next to the left. Do not pull all the way through—leave a tail of yarn hanging out the front. The length of this tail depends on how long you want your shag or fringe to be. For now, leave it on the long side (¾ of an inch is very long). It can always be cut later.

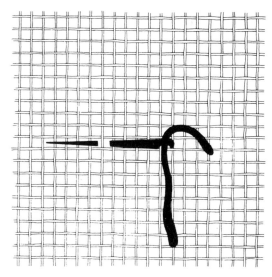

2. Reach two canvas threads straight to the right, and emerge one hole back to the left. Pull tight to hold your first tail in place. Be sure that your needle is in front of the yarn loop on the needle and does not inadvertently go through the loop.

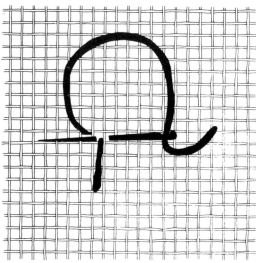

3. Again, go straight to the right across two canvas threads and emerge back one, but this time do not pull your yarn all the way through. Leave a loop of whatever size your work requires.

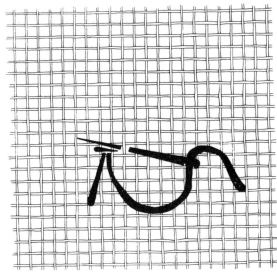

4. Again, go straight to the right across two canvas threads and back one. Pull tight to hold your previous loop in place. Be sure your needle is placed correctly as shown.

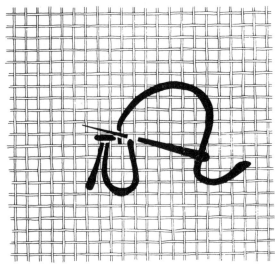

5. Repeat as before—right over two, back one, and form a loop.

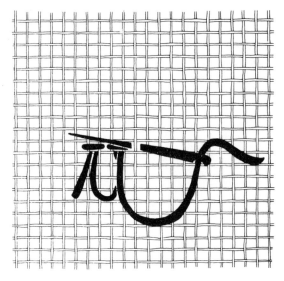

6. Again, right over two, back one, and now pull tight. Learn the rhythm.

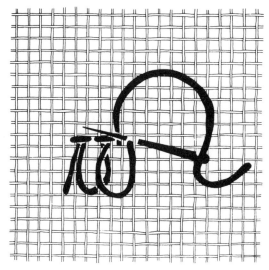

7. You can use this loopy fringe either in the heart of your work or around the border, or cut it as long or short as you like.

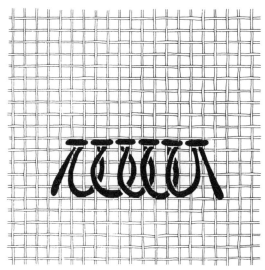

8. Start your second row directly above the first. Loops tend to lie downward, so it is difficult to work *under* a finished row. However, when you have completed your work in this stitch, push all your loops upward for the best effect.

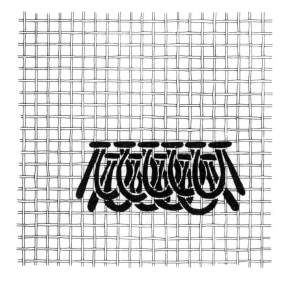

Weaving

This stitch formation is attractive and nicely textured. It does not cover the canvas well and, therefore, cannot take a good deal of wear, but it is an excellent filler where an interesting woven basket pattern can show up to good advantage. Compensation is not too difficult, but it may look conspicuous if used too extensively.

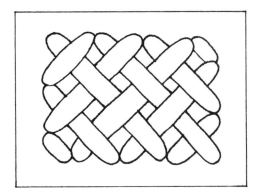

1. The first and the last rows of this formation are made up entirely of compensating stitches. Begin one canvas thread down from the upper right-hand corner of the area to be worked. Pull your yarn through the darkened hole. Slant up and over one intersection of canvas threads to the left, and then slant down to the left one intersection and emerge.

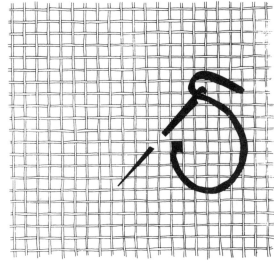

2. Again slant up and over one canvas thread to the left. Emerge down and under one canvas thread to the left.

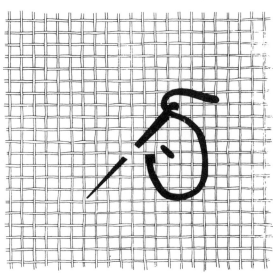

3. Continue in this manner, forming small backward slanting stitches.

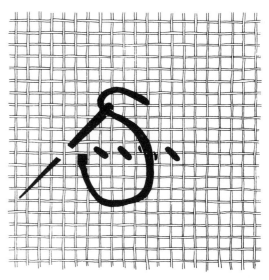

4. At the left-hand border of your work, begin the second row by emerging two canvas threads straight down after completing your last stitch. This will put you in position to begin your next row.

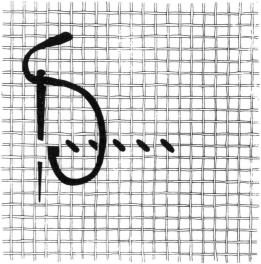

5. Reach up and over *two* intersections of canvas threads to the right, sharing a hole, and emerge straight down two canvas threads.

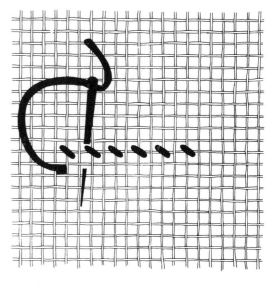

6. Again, reach up and over two intersections to the right, sharing a hole. Emerge straight down two canvas threads. Continue across the row.

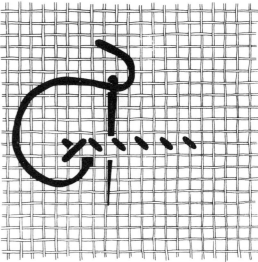

7. Work the final stitch of this row by reaching up and over only *one* intersection, sharing a hole, and once again emerge straight down two canvas threads.

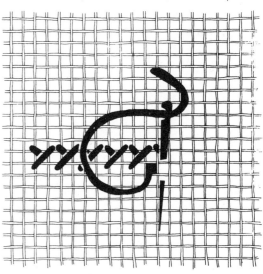

8. Now diagonal to the left, up and over two intersections. Do not pull this stitch over on top of your previous long diagonal stitch, but rather push that stitch aside to make room for this one. Emerge two canvas threads straight down.

9. Note that each row ends with a small compensating stitch.

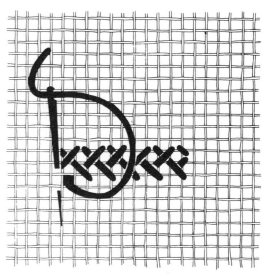

10. Moving back to the right again, you will slant to the right up and over two canvas intersections again, not going on top of, but pushing aside, the stitch from your previous row in order to share a hole with a stitch that is slanting in the same direction.

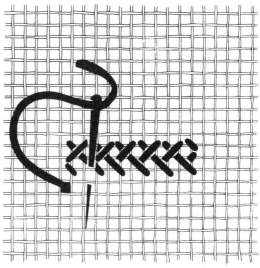

11. As your work progresses, you will see a weaving pattern emerge. This diagram shows how to begin your final compensating row. Instead of reaching down two threads after your last small slanting stitch, as you have been doing at the end of each row, this time you must angle back into the hole just vacated. Reach up to the left over one intersection of canvas threads, slanting down one intersection to the left to emerge.

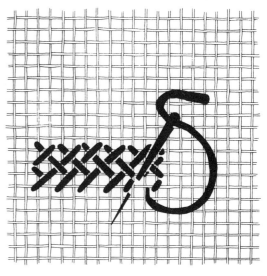

12. Continue your last row with small slanting stitches that cover only one intersection of canvas threads. If your final compensating row is moving to the left, your little stitches will slant to the left as did your first compensating row. But if your final row (which must always compensate) is moving to the right, your last compensating row will be made up of small slanting stitches pointing in that direction.

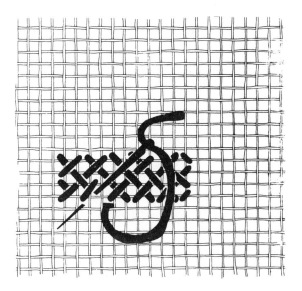

PART TWO

Projects

Introduction to Projects

In this section I have tried to give the reader a wide selection of delicacies to suit the taste of the most exacting palate. The many different styles and shapes of design in these projects will hopefully catch every needlepointer from the most traditional-minded to the most contemporary in my net.

As those who know of my teaching are aware, I do not believe in presenting projects with "the briefest possible" descriptions and instructions. The stitches used in these projects have already been shown in diagrams and explained in text in Part One of the book. Where I felt that an individual stitch or its special usage presented a problem, I have added extra diagrams within this project section. Where I thought that words alone might not convey a complicated procedure to everyone, I have added additional illustrations. The first page of each project shows a line drawing of the completed design, and there is also a color photograph of each project (see Color Plates 1–23) to help you with color or stitch effect.

I know many people will be glad that I have also supplied the yarn amounts—in every color—necessary to complete each project. As for general supplies, I do recommend that the avid needlepointer keep on hand pencils, graph paper (both the large 17- by 22-inch pads and the smaller type of pad that is divided by a heavier blue line into 10- by 10-hole squares), a can of clear acrylic spray, #18, #20, and #13 (quickpoint) needles, perhaps a yard each of mono 10, 12, and 14 canvas, tracing paper, and, of course, small sharp-pointed scissors. I wear these around my neck attached to a decorative tape measure which is enormously handy.

If a particular design catches your eye, but you would prefer to use it in a different form, I urge you to experiment with it. Try new stitches or colors. Try the Wallpaper-Motif Vest design as a pillow. Try the Decorative Panel design as a vest.

It is my experience that frequently the greatest contribution an author can make is to plant a seed that may blossom into something quite different and original. It is this type of experience that gives the reader the greatest pride and satisfaction, so it is my hope that within this section lie many seeds waiting to sprout.

Working from a Painted Canvas

First of all, why should you work from a painted canvas? Is it possible to do so and still be creative? Of course it is. But I feel that the best reason for working from a painted canvas is because the artwork is often so delightful that it is irresistible. After all, even an artist buys art!

A painted canvas also makes things easier in some ways because much of the initial planning is done for you. There is no need to count stitches as you do when working from a graph, and broad color selections are already made. But where then is the creativity? Ah—a painted canvas may be the greatest challenge to your imagination, because creativity lies in the subtle choices that you make. If orange is called for, which orange will set off the brown? Should it be the salmon or the coral or the brilliant clear orange of Halloween? When working this or that line (the paint rarely falls exactly on a single canvas thread), one must decide whether this stitch will look best as part of the white background or the pink flower. You must decide if the roundness of the petal should be emphasized or if it would look better cut off more sharply. It is a small touch, but important.

And then there is the matter of which stitches to use. Should this area be raised? Should this lie flat? Would a small area require too much compensation to be effective in this or that stitch?

I have seen many painted canvases start out as identical, and end up being charming reflections of the different personalities and tastes of the people who worked them.

In the realm of the purely technical, be as sure as possible that the color on the canvas is fast and the canvas mesh is of good quality. How can you be sure? Buy good quality and ask if there is a guarantee of colorfastness. Beware of too great a bargain. If your canvas runs during blocking, or if the mesh softens to a point where the holes are uneven and almost impossible to locate, you will have wasted hours of patient effort and fond hopes. (See "Questions and Answers: Canvas" for more information in this area.)

Harper's Lady

COLOR PLATES 1 AND 2 AND JACKET COVER

I love to design my own canvases, especially when new ideas evolve from objects around me that are unrelated to needlepoint. But sometimes I run across a painted canvas design that is so appealing I cannot resist it. This design was just such a case. I wanted to experiment with the effects of a variety of stitches on the pattern. You will find where to obtain this and other lively magazine cover canvases in the "Shopping Guide."

MATERIALS

Needle: #18 tapestry type.

Canvas: 12 mono canvas. The finished size is about 12 by 16 inches.

Persian yarn: You will need the following colors and quantities.
Dark yellow—9 yards or ¼ ounce.
Light yellow—9 yards or ¼ ounce.
Dark green—5 yards or ¼ ounce.
Light green—9 yards or ¼ ounce.
Dark gray—45 yards or ¾ ounce.
Light gray—15 yards or ¼ ounce.
Dark pink—15 yards or ¼ ounce.
Light pink—60 yards or 1 ounce.
Dark orange—5 yards or ¼ ounce.
Light orange—5 yards or ¼ ounce.
White yarn (background)—215 yards or 4 ounces.

Silk yarn: You'll need a bit of white for the hat.

Velvet yarn: Velura is a nice texture for parts of the flowers. It is usually sold on cards of about 10 yards. Try some orange and pink.

GETTING STARTED

Use 2-ply strands of your Persian yarn for this design (peel off a single ply from each length, then combine these extras to make new 2-ply strands) except for the Algerian Eye stitch, which takes only a single ply.

First you'll work the face, neck, and upper brim and crown of the hat in either the Continental or Basketweave. I always prefer the Basketweave for solid areas. Next, outline the coat in the Continental stitch (you can't use the Basketweave for a single row of outline). Work the inner brim of the hat in the Pulled-Thread stitch to simulate straw in an open weave. Work the bulk of the coat in a Gobelin

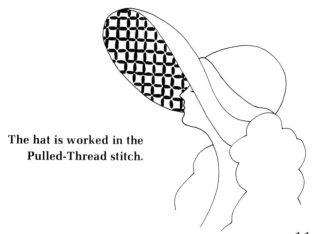

The hat is worked in the Pulled-Thread stitch.

variation (see the Gobelin stitch, Diagrams 7 and 8) to get a tweedy look. This is quick and easy, and it works wonders to give the model a high-fashion look. Next work the collar in Turkey Knots to give the effect of fur.

Use the Cross-Box stitch for the bright yellow corners, and Flat stitch variation of the Scotch stitch (see Diagram 9) for the dark orange. Where these stitches didn't fit exactly, I used compensating stitches as described in the final diagrams for most of the stitches in this book. The inner background is worked in the Smyrna Double-Cross over four meshes. Be sure not to use too heavy a yarn or the intricacies of the stitch will get lost. A 2-ply strand is surely enough in Persian. (Try a single ply to see if it covers.) Compensate along the sides of the design and along the figure (see Diagram 7 of the Smyrna Double-Cross).

FINISHING

I have chosen to display this work in a simple chrome frame, but it works up into a stunning pillow as well. If you prefer a pillow, I would suggest a box-edged type so your lady does not get pulled back at the corners as would happen with a knife-edged pillow. See the chapter on "Blocking and Finishing" for further instructions.

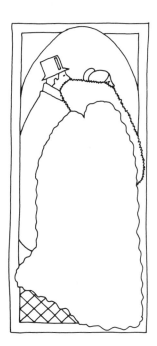

On the Town

This is another painted canvas that I could not resist. It could have been worked entirely in the Basketweave or Continental, but I saw such exciting possibilities for a number of decorative stitches that I had to try them out. Here is the result. You can find out how to obtain this canvas from the "Shopping Guide," and if you want to work yours just like mine, this is how you go about it.

MATERIALS

Needle: # 18 or # 20 tapestry type.

Canvas: 14 mono mesh. The finished size is about 6 by 12 inches.

Persian yarn: You'll need the following colors and quantities. *Black*—80 yards or 1½ ounces. *Yellow*—25 yards or ½ ounce. *Orange*—1 strand. *Dark blue*—20 yards or ½ ounce. *Light blue*—20 yards or ½ ounce. *White*—240 yards or 4 ounces (for the luxurious fur coat). *Brown*—1 strand. *Gray*—1 strand.

Silk yarn or cotton floss: 2 yards of a flesh-tone color.

Velvet yarn: 19 yards of navy blue Velura.

Metallic yarn: 10 yards of gold.

GETTING STARTED

Follow the colors painted on the canvas. If you have trouble obtaining any of the specialty yarns, the "Shopping Guide" will tell you where you might write for them. But if you do not wish to take the time or trouble, this canvas will still look quite effective if worked just in Persian and the gold metallic yarn. Use the Basketweave or Continental stitches if not otherwise specified.

Work the faces first in silk or cotton floss, then the hair. Work the black section of the man's hat in a small Cross stitch over two meshes, and the white highlight in Continental. Next, outline the lady's coat in Continental, and then work the man's coat with navy blue velvet yarn in the Knitting stitch. The bit of white around the collar will be Continental.

Using first the gold metallic thread and then the black yarn for alternate squares, work the lower right-hand corner, filling the squares with a loose and flexible variation of the Scotch stitch. Start with 2-, 4-, and 6-mesh stitches and work stitches as large as necessary

———— Gold ▬▬▬ Black

The Scotch stitch variation for
On the Town. Work stitches over two, four,
six, eight, ten, twelve, and fourteen threads,
and then decrease in sequence.

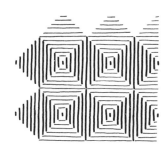

to reach out to the points of the squares and then decrease in sequence. As this canvas is silk-screened, the squares may not always be uniform.

The lady's coat should be worked in a high Turkey Knot stitch. Leave the loops uncut. Her collar is worked in close French Knots of Persian yarn. The pale blue ground under the man's coat is worked in Continental or Basketweave. Finally, work the upper gold metallic section in Basketweave and the arch in the Pulled-Thread stitch to resemble tiny panes of glass. All else is Basketweave.

FINISHING

First I blocked this piece right side up (water does not damage the metallic yarn) and then I had it commercially mounted on a piece of wallboard that had a cutout in the back to allow light to show through the Pulled-Thread stitches. Any framing store should be able to do this for you, or you might be able to do it yourself, following the directions for framing on plywood in the "Blocking and Finishing" chapter. But in this case, before wrapping your needlepoint around the board, you would use a scroll saw or jigsaw to cut out an arch in the upper area of your board. The piece is then hung where light from behind can shine through the small window panes. It is most effective and unusual.

116

Greenhouse

Here is another canvas that attracted me immediately. The design is marked on the canvas in outline only, with no colors painted in. The idea is to use whatever leftover yarns you have to fill in each area. It is inexpensive to purchase (see the "Shopping Guide"), and the final result is very lovely. Although the canvas comes with a small color photo suggesting how it might be worked, I have chosen to do it with a wide variety of decorative stitches and brilliantly colored flowers. As before, where I do not specify a particular stitch, use the Basketweave or Continental.

MATERIALS

Needle: #18 tapestry type.

Canvas: 12 mono canvas. The finished size is about 10 by 22 inches.

Persian yarn: You will need a total of about 450 yards or 7½ ounces. *Black*—70 yards or 1¼ ounces. *Brick red*—120 yards or 2 ounces. *Dark turquoise*—60 yards or 1 ounce. *Light turquoise*—120 yards or 2 ounces. *White*—80 yards or 1½ ounces. *Dark rust*—12 yards or ¼ ounce. *Left-hand flowerpot*—about 7 yards of different shades of pink for each coral leaf, and 10 yards of green for the green buds. *Middle flowerpot*—about 12 yards for each fern frond in a medley of greens. *Right-hand flowerpot*—about 9 yards of varied moss greens for each leaf. Pansies will each use about 4 yards of petal color, 2 yards of yellow, and 3 yards of black.

GETTING STARTED

Use any leftover colors that you like for your flowers; the leaves and fronds can be a collection of various greens. The background around the pots, as well as the trellis, can be any light color. In estimating, I have given you a good deal more yarn than you will actually need—so even if you decide to rip here or there, you should not run short. Use 2-ply yarn except for the bricks and the pansies, which will all use full 3-ply strands of Persian yarn.

Work the trellis in the Weaving and Knitting stitches.

The bricks are filled in first with large straight Gobelin stitches that vary in size to fit the shape of each brick. The black mortar around the bricks is worked next in a Basketweave or Continental stitch. The white slats of the trellis that slant down to the left are worked in the Weaving stitch, while the slats moving down to the right are worked in the Knitting stitch. All the flowerpots have outlines and dark shaded areas that are worked in Basketweave or Continental. The larger parts of the body of each pot are worked in a horizontal Gobelin over two meshes, and the rims in a vertical Gobelin over two meshes.

For the flowerpot on the left, work the leaves in several shades of coral and pink in the Basketweave or Continental, and work the

117

green buds below in French Knots. The flowerpot in the center has fern fronds all worked in Basketweave or Continental, with a single line of uneven straight Gobelin stitches outlining the center ridge of the two upper fronds. The third flowerpot has all its leaves worked in the Basketweave or Continental using bits and pieces of leftover greens. The black centers of the two pansies on the left are worked in Turkey Knots, the loops of which are then cut. The pink and purple areas of two of the pansies are worked in a small Brick stitch (over two meshes). The rest of the flowers are worked in the Basketweave or Continental, as is the area around all the flowerpots. The sharp-eyed reader may notice that I added three little French Knots nestled in the leaves under the turquoise flower.

FINISHING

I selected a dark wood deep-set frame, as I wished this piece to hang in an old farmhouse. But a chrome frame chosen for a modern kitchen or any sunny room would also be appropriate, If you wish to use this design for a pillow, it should first be blocked and then mounted into a box-edged pillow, perhaps with black piping to match the mortar.

Tracing Your Own Design

Why trace your own design when there are so many lovely designs on the market? Because sometimes you find exactly what you want to needlepoint on a record cover, in a magazine, or on a scrap of wallpaper. Or perhaps you want to copy your own drapery fabric for a needlepoint cushion or dining-room chair seat. Or you may wish to copy a favorite drawing or work a portrait of a friend or relative.

There is also a great deal of satisfaction in taking something from one medium and transforming it into another. Bette Midler looks very handsome in needlepoint!

Moreover, tracing is easy and inexpensive. Basically it requires only a pencil in addition to your usual needlepoint supplies of needle, yarn, and canvas. You simply place your mesh on top of the design to be traced and copy the outlines with your pencil. The size mesh you use will be largely determined by the complexity of the design being traced. The more intricate the design, the finer your canvas must be to encompass all the detail.

If you plan to work a design on fine mesh, you may prefer to trace it on tracing paper first with a fairly heavy Magic Marker (which you will not use on the mesh). Then trace the design with a #2 pencil or permanent marker on to the canvas. It will probably be easier to see these heavy lines through the fine mesh than it would be to see the original design. (See "Questions and Answers: Tracing Designs," pages 10–11.)

I do not attempt to put color on my canvas when tracing. The outlines are enough. For color, I refer to the original piece from which the tracing was taken. If you are concerned that a dark yarn will not fully cover an area of unpainted canvas, you might darken this area with a colored wash of acrylic paint.

Tracing designs gives one a feeling of great accomplishment. The design itself may not be original because it was copied from something else, but the end result in needlepoint may be quite original, is frequently most effective, sometimes very amusing, and often extremely beautiful.

A Child's Sketch

COLOR PLATES 4 AND 5

My own children were too old, and my grandchildren too young, to provide me with the type of delightful naïve sketch that I had envisioned. But my godchild, Dawn Martin, sent me this one and I love it.

MATERIALS

Needle: #18 tapestry type will probably do. Look under "Questions and Answers: Needles and Yarn" for more complete information

Canvas: Generally a child's drawing has bold simple lines and translates nicely to a 10 or 12 canvas. I have used a 10 mono mesh canvas. For more specific instructions, consult "Questions and Answers: Canvas."

Persian yarn: For every square inch of an individual color, you will require roughly 2 yards of yarn in that color. Once again check the "Questions and Answers" chapter for complete directions on how to compute yarn requirements in either yards or ounces.

GETTING STARTED

To trace your design, place the canvas on top of your drawing and trace the outline with a pencil. Use a #2 pencil, and spray the canvas with clear acrylic fixative so your pencil lines will not rub off.

If you have the original sketch beside you as you work, you can refer to it for color as you go along. If you cannot keep the original, number all your colors. Then draw a rough sketch of the original, marking the numbered yarn colors in the proper place so you will know where to use each color as you proceed.

Begin with the areas defined by a single line. These are the most important for establishing a likeness to the original. Even where there are blocks of solid color, I believe it is best to outline first to be sure the result is pleasing. If you feel that one stitch or another should be moved or a line lengthened or shortened, it is easier to do now when there is very little ripping involved.

I did this particular work completely in Basketweave because I wanted to preserve the flat look of the original. First I worked the lettering and then the little girl with her balloons.

If your sketch lends itself to decorative stitchery, there is no reason not to use it. If your design includes animals of some sort, it would be delightful to make "fur" in the French Knot or Turket Knot, and other decorative stitches might be used elsewhere.

FINISHING

A simple frame of painted or unpainted wood or even a chrome frame is suitable. Your sketch could be matted first if you like. Needlepoint does not generally need glass over it, but if you want to use glass I strongly recommend the nonglare type.

Your drawing can also be blocked and made into a charming pillow. Or it could be mounted on the front of a canvas or leather tote bag. But it will last longest if it is framed and hung on the wall, out of harm's way.

Floral Fabric Pillow

For this project, I selected a medium-priced Schumacher 100 percent cotton, glazed chintz, which can have a matching laminated wallpaper (see the "Shopping Guide"). It is available in several color combinations, including bright tones of pink and green. For this project, however, I decided to use earth tones. A beautiful room could be planned by using the wallpaper on your walls and the fabric at the windows. A solid color from the design (chocolate brown, burnt orange, or olive green) might be used to cover large chairs, a sofa, or a bed. Chair seats could be worked in needlepoint by tracing the pattern, and pillows might also be made in the large size as shown or in smaller individual squares.

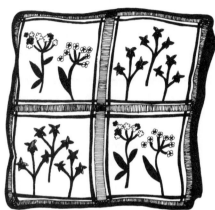

The design would also lend itself to a valance across the window, or, worked in separate squares, to a magnificent rug or wallhanging. Eight full designs, sewn together, would make a rug roughly 3 by 6 feet. This design could also be worked in quickpoint, using 5-mesh-to-the-inch rug canvas and rug yarns. For the same amount of effort, you would then have a rug twice the size and tough as iron. For a rug strong enough to be walked on, work entirely in Basketweave.

MATERIALS

Needle: #18 tapestry type.

Canvas: ⅔ yard 10 mono mesh. The finished pillow size is about 18 by 18 inches.

Persian yarn: I was not able to match the colors of the fabric exactly, but I came close enough. As usual, I allowed two yards of yarn to the square inch in the following colors. *Black*—45 yards or ¾ ounce. *Earth brown*—90 yards or 1½ ounces. *Dark brown*—13 yards or ¼ ounce. *Beige*—58 yards or 1 ounce. *Burnt orange*—30 yards or ½ ounce. *Light orange*—25 yards or ½ ounce. *Dark gray*—12 yards or ¼ ounce. *Light gray*—16 yards or ½ ounce. *Green*—60 yards or ¾ ounce. *Off-white (background)*—330 yards or 5½ ounces.

GETTING STARTED

Spread your fabric out on a level table, holding or securing it as taut as possible. Place your canvas on top and trace the design with a #2 pencil (spray with fixative so the lines will not rub off). For straight lines, such as those used around the borders of each square, I noted the approximate placement of these lines, and then simply drew straight across a row of my canvas. Mesh is never perfectly square, nor can you hold it perfectly straight, so it is difficult if not outright impossible to *trace* an absolutely straight line. Therefore, it is always best when tracing a pattern to locate whatever straight lines there may be, and *draw* them in along a row or track to give you a point of reference for the balance of the design.

The brown and beige borders of this pattern, you will notice, are wobbly and uneven on the fabric. I decided not to attempt to capture this effect. Unless I were using a very fine canvas (perhaps an 18 mesh), my lines would appear stepped, not wavy. This would, I feel, make the entire piece look stiff instead of flowing and casual. Therefore, I drew straight lines on the canvas rather than tracing the wavy ones. In spite of this deviation, I believe that the feel and the charm of the original design are intact.

It is important for your peace of mind to remember that needlepoint is worked on a material that is made up of small, square, open boxes. Unless your design has a geometric look perfectly suited to these boxes, it is likely that your design will *not* accommodate itself exactly to this material. So try for a good likeness rather than for perfection when copying any design. The eye of the beholder will do the rest. The only truly perfect copying jobs are done by machines, which is one reason why handwork is always so much more interesting. It is *imperfect.* Check a fine Persian rug sometime, and note how unevenly placed and unevenly shaped the "matching" motifs really are.

Trace the rest of the pillow as near to the original as possible. Begin your needlepoint by working first the outer and then the inner borders. The outer border is worked in a straight Gobelin stitch over seven canvas threads. The inner border is worked in the Greek stitch over three meshes. For the center and corner blocks, I used single Cross-Box stitches worked over seven-by-seven meshes. The white area between the dark and light brown borders is the slanted Gobelin stitch. The flowers are worked next, and finally the background.

As your background will be light, be careful not to leave any dark ends of yarn from your flowers hanging down in the back; they might get caught up in the white and show through as dark shadows. Weave these hanging ends under in back and snip off any excess.

The background is worked in the Byzantine stitch over two meshes. Begin in the upper left-hand corner of each square and work nine

Here is a keyed stitch chart.

1 Slanted Gobelin
2 Gobelin
3 Byzantine
4 Basketweave
5 Cross-Box
6 Greek

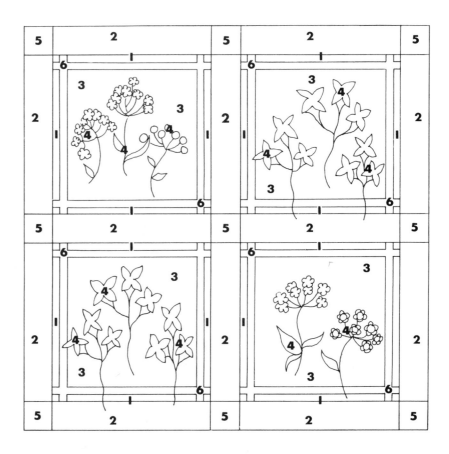

stitches to a row before changing direction. When you meet an obstruction, stop and compensate with a small single stitch as illustrated in the stitch diagrams. Remember not to count your compensating stitch as one of the nine, but when working the Byzantine, the last full stitch going in one direction always counts as the first stitch in the next direction.

Whenever the Byzantine had to be interrupted to accommodate the flowers, I tried to figure out exactly where it would pick up again on the other side of the flowers by counting the mesh. I proved to be more often wrong than right as I discovered later, but it's difficult to detect the ten-stitch row or the eight-stitch row that occurs here and there.

In between the flowers, where the use of the Byzantine would have required far too much compensation, I simply worked the Basketweave or the Continental. It looks just fine.

Background:

• **Basketweave**

╱ **Byzantine**

Flowers:

╱ **Basketweave (black)**

✕ **Basketweave (brown)**

○ **Basketweave (green)**

This graph shows the stitches used for the flowers and the spaces in between.

If I had been using this design for a rug or chair seat, it would have been best to work the entire piece in the Basketweave, as decorative stitches will tend to pull up and will not wear as well as the smaller, tighter Basketweave stitch. But the decorative stitches are fine for a wallhanging, pillow, or valance.

FINISHING

First my work was blocked. Then, using a dark-brown velvet for the reverse side, I had the pillow made up with a box edge and piping. (Suede or Ultrasuede would also be lovely for this pillow.) The use of a box edge instead of a knife edge ensures that the corners of the pillow will not slope back but will sit flat.

Copyright © 1972 Atlantic Recording Corporation
Cover design by Richard Amsel

Bette Midler Record Cover

COLOR PLATE 6

This record album cover caught my eye, and as my elder daughter is a great fan of Bette, I decided to trace the image and give it to her to work. She was thoroughly delighted and did a lovely job as you can see. The design comes from an Atlantic Record Album (SD-7238) entitled "Bette Midler—the Divine Miss M."

MATERIALS

Needle: #18 tapestry type.

Canvas: ⅔ yard 12 mono mesh. The finished size is about 17 by 10½ inches.

Persian yarn: You'll need the following colors and quantities. *Black*—4 yards or ¼ ounce. *Hot pink*—4 yards of ¼ ounce. *Medium pink*—10 yards of ¼ ounce. *Palest pink*—1 yard or ¼ ounce. *Orange*—3 yards or ¼ ounce. *Yellow*—1 yard or ¼ ounce. *Darkest brown*—5 yards or ¼ ounce. *Rust brown*—100 yards or 1¾ ounces. *Blue*—4 yards or ¼ ounce. *White*—210 yards or 3½ ounces.

GETTING STARTED

Place your canvas, centered, over the record cover, holding it as straight and taut as possible. Trace the outline in pencil or guaranteed permanent marker.

You will notice that although a record cover is about 12 by 12 inches, I decided to change the proportions of the overall canvas and made mine 17 by 10½ inches. If you wish to do the same, pencil in this rectangle on your canvas, and center Bette's face there before starting to trace her image.

It is not necessary to paint or color the canvas as the colors can be worked by following the album cover. If you are working from a borrowed cover and cannot keep it, make one tracing on your mesh as described above, and another on a piece of tracing paper. Indicate the colors on the tracing with Magic Markers or crayon for later reference.

Do the features first (eyes, nose shadow, and mouth) in Basketweave or Continental, using 2-ply strands of Persian yarn. Then work the cheeks and hair. The cheeks are worked in the Parisian stitch and the hair in the Brick stitch with a full 3-ply strand of yarn. Final curlicues of hair are worked in the Continental with a 2-ply strand.

Work the background in the Mosaic stitch (a Parisian stitch variation). Those with sharp eyes may notice that my daughter inadvertently changed the direction of her Mosaic stitches in midstream. A mistake is often the basis of a very interesting treatment.

For those who might like to deviate from this model, try working Bette's hair in the Turkey Knot, leaving the loops intact to give a really curly look. The eyelashes could also be done in the same stitch but with the loops cut, then stiffened a bit with the help of a little glue to simulate long lashes. Purchase a double amount of hair-color yarn for the Turkey Knot.

FINISHING

Bette would look great in a modern Lucite or chrome frame. Or you might try mounting her, after blocking, on a piece of plywood. This method is described in the "Blocking and Finishing" chapter. Miss M would also make a great throw pillow. I would prefer an unpiped, knife-edged cushion.

A Portrait

The high-contrast photo of Abby

Abby in needlepoint

This portrait of my youngest daughter was made from a high-contrast black-and-white photograph. The original picture, I felt, was an indifferent likeness, but the high-contrast negative made from it picked up her facial bone structure and provided an excellent likeness. I must confess that I added a few larger eyelashes, as the 12 mono mesh I used was not fine enough to pick up the tiny lash lines of the photograph. The finished piece is not a perfect likeness, as you can see by comparing the original photograph of Abby with the final needlepoint portrait, but the essential character is there, and everyone recognizes her at once and exclaims over it.

Most local photographers will be able to print this type of photographic enlargement from your negative. If you have a darkroom, you may be able to do it yourself. But if you cannot have it done locally, send it to me at In Stitches (see the "Shopping Guide") and I will try to have it done for you. But a word of caution. I have found, alas, that this technique works best for young people, as the soft "character" lines and shadows that older people acquire tend to become overemphasized in high contrast, and give a very harsh effect.

MATERIALS

Needle: #18 tapestry type.

Canvas: ⅔ yard of 12 mono mesh. The finished size of my portrait is about 13 by 16 inches.

Persian yarn: You will need a total of about 7½ ounces or 450 yards. Divide this up as necessary, allowing 2 yards of color per square inch, and 60 yards to an ounce.

GETTING STARTED

Obtain an 11-by-14-inch high-contrast photographic enlargement. In my portrait, Abby's face measured approximately 9 by 9 inches and was centered in the enlargement, but this is not absolutely necessary. You might prefer a profile off-center, for instance.

Holding your mesh as straight and taut as possible, place it over the photograph and trace the black portions with a pencil or guaranteeed permanent marking pen, (See "Questions and Answers: Marking Canvas" to see what type of markers are acceptable.) Do not fill in the black areas, simply outline them, keeping your canvas extremely taut to avoid distortion. If you have a plywood board, it might be best to staple down both photograph and canvas before tracing, as the slightest distortion here will make a great difference in your final likeness. If you have used a pencil, it would be best to spray it with a

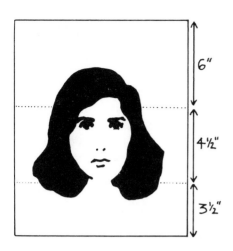

6"

4½"

3½"

This is one way to work the background: use three bands of color, such as medium-dark blue, medium blue, and pale blue, that will show up against the white.

clear acrylic fixative spray to be sure that it does not come off on your white yarn as you work.

This entire portrait was worked in Basketweave or Continental. Start with the features and hair. Then fill in the background, being sure you have not left any ends of black yarn hanging in back that might get caught up in the white and show through as dark shadows. Any yarn tails should be woven in and out of the back of your work and then snipped off close.

If you prefer, the background could be worked in one of the decorative stitches (Smyrna Double-Cross, Leaf, Milanese, Byzantine, Scotch, or Knitting). The hair and lashes, of course, could be worked in Turkey Knots or French Knots for a very curly effect.

I decided to plot out Abby's name and add it to the background. I worked out her name as four rows of simple block letters. Each row covers the previous row a bit, in an ever-darker shade. This gives the impression that the letters are moving forward toward the viewer.

Planning the letters so they will fit evenly takes a great deal of counting, and as the eagle-eyed among you may note, I did not get it exactly right. But no matter. I love the final effect.

An interesting effect can also be achieved by filling in the background with three large bands of color. For example, you could use a dark band about 6 inches wide across the top, another lighter band about 4½ inches wide below it, and a final band in the palest shade, about 3½ inches wide along the bottom.

FINISHING

I chose a stark black mat, 3 inches wide, to set off the portrait, and put it in a simple chrome frame. This gave a modern bold effect. If you prefer a softer, more traditional look, you might use a pale mat and a distressed wood frame.

127

Child's Director's Chairs

COLOR PLATE 15

Children love these charming chairs, and this project is fun to work and not too difficult to mount. It does require a bit of thought and planning in order to correctly center the numbers in the circles and fit the blocks on the back. Of the two versions pictured, the clown is worked on a 12 mesh and the furry animal on a 5 quickpoint mesh. You can find out where to get the chairs from the "Shopping Guide," and if you are the least bit handy with a sewing machine, you can probably mount the seat and back yourself.

It is best to purchase the chair before getting started, as the seat must be worked to the exact edges of the frame. The needlepoint is too thick to allow the chair to fold over on top of it, so at the far sides you must work one row at a time toward the edge to ensure a perfect fit. Moreover, every chair is somewhat different in size.

Clown Design

MATERIALS

Needle: #18 tapestry type.

Canvas: 1 yard of 36-inch-wide 12 mono mesh.

Persian yarn: The backrest of the chair requires a total of 325 yards or 5½ ounces. *Each lettered block uses the following amounts. Darkest color*—3 yards or ¼ ounce. *Medium color*—6 yards or ¼ ounce. *Light color*—4 yards or ¼ ounce. *Background*—This will amount to the balance of your total, i.e., 325 yards minus the number of yards used to work your blocks.

Persian yarn: The seat of the chair requires a total of about 325 yards or 5½ ounces. *Each circle uses the following amounts. Number*—3 yards or ¼ ounce. *Circle background*—5 yards or ¼ ounce.

Persian yarn: The requirements for the clown face are as follows. *Dark pink*—1 yard or ¼ ounce. *Light pink*—12 yards or ¼ ounce. *Yellow*—8 yards or ¼ ounce. *Dark blue*—4 yards or ¼ ounce. *Light blue*—4 yards or ¼ ounce. *Green*—3 yards or ¼ ounce.

GETTING STARTED

Begin with the backrest portion of the chair. Cut a piece of canvas measuring about 30 by 10 inches, and bind the edges with masking tape if you are not using lock-weave canvas. Leaving 2 inches all around, pencil in a rectangle 26 by 6 inches. Inside this rectangle, and centered properly, pencil in two lines, one at each far side to represent the measurement of the *front* of the backrest. The remainder wraps around and will not be seen. My two chairs, ordered from the same source, measured quite differently, so it is important to get the correct side-to-side measure of each chair. If, for instance, you find that your chair width is 16 inches, pencil in lines 5 inches on each side measuring from the far ends so your inner rectangle will be 16 by 6 inches. Spray with fixative to keep the pencil from coming off on your yarn, or use a guaranteed permanent marking pen.

All stitches on this mesh use 2-ply yarn, except for the Turkey Knot, which uses a full 3-ply strand. The blocks worked on the back can contain the child's name, but could also spell out "A B C" or the child's initials. If you plan to use just three blocks, center the inner rectangle on your canvas over one of the blocks in the illustration on page 129. Trace your middle block first, and then, moving your canvas, trace the same block on either side, making sure that these are roughly the same distance from the center block. Vary the angle and tilt of the blocks (see page 129) so the shaded areas appear on different sides. If you wish to spell out a name, work the blocks out carefully on

128

Black—3 yards or ¼ ounce.
Orange—25 yards or ½ ounce.
Red—24 yards or ½ ounce.
Aquamarine (background)—210 yards or 3½ ounces.

graph paper first. Allowing for some space on the far sides of the blocks before the wraparound, estimate the total number of canvas threads needed for your blocks. "Nathaniel," the name of my grandson, is uncommonly long and was quite a challenge. It required all sorts of slanting blocks in order to fit. "John" or "Ann" would be much easier! When you have graphed your blocks, graph the letters inside as well, again counting the meshes to be sure that your letters are centered.

**Here are some angles
to use for the blocks.**

When you have worked the needlepoint letters in your blocks, fill in the background with Basketweave or Continental. Use any colors you like for the blocks, but keep in mind that the slanting top and sides of each block should be at least two and four shades darker than the face.

For the seat of the chair, cut the remaining canvas to 15 by 19 inches and bind the edges with masking tape. Pencil in a rectangle roughly the size of your chair seat. Center this over the clown face on page 130, and trace it with a #2 pencil or guaranteed permanent marking pen. Hold your canvas straight and taut as you work. If you like, you can also trace the four bouncing balls in each corner (see the circle illustration below). I worked a number in each of these to signify the year of birth. Graph the numbers, or pencil them in freehand, centering them in the circles. Fix the pencil lines with acrylic spray.

Work the outlines, and then fill in the face with Basketweave or Continental. Add tufts of hair on either side in the Turkey Knot, using

The block and circle from the clown canvas

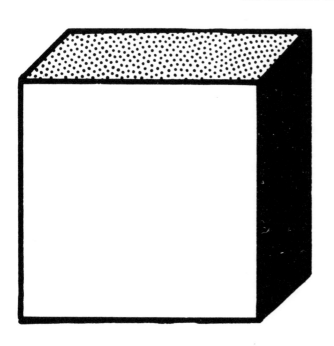 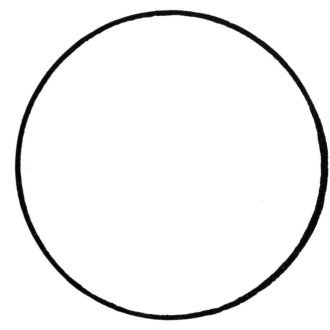

129

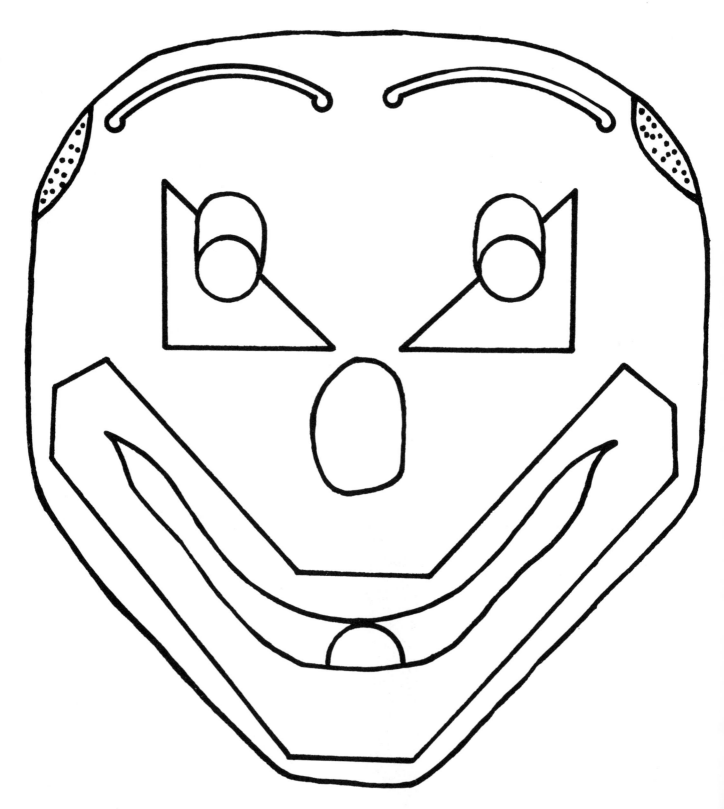

Trace the clown face from this drawing.

3-ply yarn and making the loops about 1¼ inches high. Work sixteen stitches to a side before cutting the loops. Work the circle outlines and then the number outlines before filling in. In this way you can check shapes and centering, and if you find yourself a bit off, there will not be too much to rip.

Work the background in the small Upright Cross stitch over two meshes. Start at the center and work out. As you near the sides, measure often to ensure a perfect fit. Use only 2-ply or even 1-ply if you find it will cover.

Mounting directions are on page 133 at the end of this project.

Furry Animal Design

GETTING STARTED

For the backrest of the chair, follow the directions on cutting and planning given for the clown design. If you wish to graph a full name in blocks, remember that with this larger canvas you have only about seventy canvas threads from side to side. Measure the width of your chair and multiply the number of inches by five to find out exactly how many canvas threads you have. Then graph the blocks and letters. These blocks will most probably have to be larger than the clown blocks in order to accommodate the lettering. If you plan to work about four or five blocks across the back, you can trace the block below, again varying the angle of each block.

Work the blocks in Basketweave or Continental. Then work the background in the Diagonal Cross stitch over one mesh. Make stripes two rows wide, first working two rows of dark coral, then two rows of light coral, then two rows of dark orange, and finally two rows of light orange. Then repeat.

The block for the furry animal chair

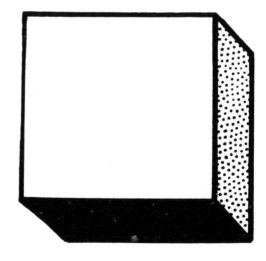

MATERIALS

Needle: #13 tapestry type or blunt-pointed knitter's needle.

Canvas: 1 yard of 5 mesh Penelope or mono rug canvas, 36 inches wide.

Rug yarn: Amounts given are for this heavier type of yarn, but you can substitute double strands of Persian yarn if you wish. Two full 3-ply strands are generally enough, but if this does not cover in some colors, you may want to use extra strands. For the chair seat you will need the following amounts. *Mauve* 1 yard or ¼ ounce. *Pink*—1 yard or ¼ ounce. *Dark green*—2 yards or ¼ ounce. *Light green*—2 yards or ¼ ounce. *Yellow*—12 yards or 1 ounce. *Dark brown*—9 yards or 1 ounce. *Light brown*—14 yards or 1 ounce. *Light gray*—6 yards of ½ ounce. *White*—12 yards or 1 ounce.

Background for the whole chair. *Dark coral*—40 yards or 2½ ounces. *Light coral*—40 yards or 2½ ounces. *Dark orange*—40 yards or 2½ ounces. *Light orange*—40 yards or 2½ ounces.

For the backrest of the chair, you will need these additional amounts. *Face of each block*—4 yards or ¼ ounce. *Top of block*—2 yards or ¼ ounce. *Side of block*—2 yards or ¼ ounce. *Letter in block*—3 yards or ¼ ounce.

The blocks can be worked in any colors that you choose, but be sure that the back and sides provide sufficient contrast from the front to show up clearly.

131

Trace the furry animal from this drawing.

After tracing the animal move the canvas so the flower fits on the stem, and trace the flower.

For the seat of the chair, pencil in a rectangle that roughly corresponds to the size of the seat of your chair. Place your mesh over the drawing of the furry animal on page 132 and trace it neatly in the center of your rectangle.

Work the flower and the entire animal (except for the tufts in the ears and on the chest), in Basketweave or Continental. The tufts should be worked in the Turkey Knot stitch. Keep the loops short, then cut and fluff when finished. Work the background in Diagonal Cross stitch stripes in the same way as for the backrest. Start at the center and work out, measuring frequently as you near the sides.

After blocking, measure again to be sure of a perfect fit. If necessary, add (or rip!) stitches after blocking.

FINISHING

Block your pieces and make sure that the seat portion reaches just to (but not beyond) the side frame of your chair. Cut the raw canvas edges to ¾ of an inch from your work all around. Cut across the corners so the flaps fold back smoothly. Turn back the canvas edges sharply and steam press them firmly.

Unfold the chair and remove the canvas seat and back. Use a sewing machine (or sew by hand) to stitch the needlepoint directly to the original chair canvas on four sides of the seat and along the top, bottom, and sides of the backrest, following the canvas pattern on top and bottom. Fit the back on the chair and adjust the chair to full size.

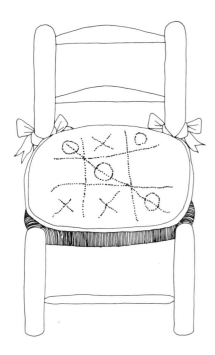

Tic-Tac-Toe Doorstop

COLOR PLATE 13

The secret of this little doorstop is in the mounting. Miniature chairs are generally available (see the "Shopping Guide"), but they must be weighted to stop a door effectively. I do this by filling my inner pillow form with sand or small iron weights, much like a bean bag. (See the "Blocking and Finishing" chapter for more details on making up your little chair seat.) I used a tic-tac-toe design, but any small, simple motif can be used effectively. You may want to design or adapt something of your own.

MATERIALS

Needle: #18 tapestry type.

Canvas: 12 mono mesh, cut 2 inches larger on all sides than the chair seat to be fitted.

Persian yarn: You'll need the following amounts for the tic-tac-toe design in a finished size of 5½ by 5½ inches: *White*—8 yards or ¼ ounce. *Pink*—60 yards or 1 ounce.

GETTING STARTED

Place the canvas on top of the design on page 135 and trace it with a #2 pencil or gray permanent marker. When using white yarn over pencil, it is always best to spray the lines with an acrylic fixative so the pencil will not rub off on your yarn. Draw in an approximate outline for the seat area of the chair.

Work the tic-tac-toe design first in the Continental stitch, using a 2-ply strand of yarn. Next, preferably working in Basketweave, fill in your background. Work from the center portion out, and fit your canvas on your chair often as you near the outer edges.

When you feel you have achieved a good fit, block your canvas and fold back the raw edges. Now see if the seat fits properly or if it needs a bit of adding, ripping, or reshaping. If it is not exactly right, make the appropriate changes and re-block. If you have worked too far in some areas, it may be possible simply to turn back the surplus needlepoint instead of ripping it.

FINISHING

Make the seat up into a fat little knife-edged pillow. Pipe and back the pillow with a pretty fabric. You might also want to sew two little ribbon ties on the back of your cushion so you can tie it on to the chair. See the "Blocking and Finishing" chapter for instructions on making a knife-edged cushion. If you wish to use the chair as a doorstop, weight the little cushion with sand, small iron weights, or even pebbles. Or, the "Shopping Guide" will advise where a similar but

Trace the tic-tac-toe design from this drawing.

dark wood little chair already weighted can be obtained. This type does not have a rush seat, but rather a muslin seat awaiting a needlepoint cover.

Wallpaper-Motif Vest

COLOR PLATES 12 AND 13

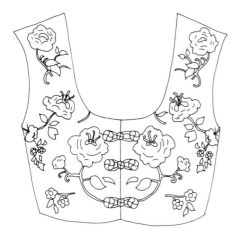

The design for this lovely vest was borrowed from an old scrap of wallpaper. It looks beautiful worn with a long evening skirt, dressy slacks, or an afternoon skirt. The illustrations provide elements of the wallpaper design that can be traced in any arrangement you choose. But you may prefer to select and adapt your own wallpaper or a fabric (scarves are a particularly rich source of vibrant design). This chapter will tell you how to go about working your vest. With a vest or any piece of clothing, it is quite important that you use the Basketweave. The Continental will pull the design so badly out of shape that it will be difficult if not impossible to match your two sides later. However, if you must use the Continental, be sure to follow the special directions that accompany the Continental stitch instruction diagrams on pages 39–40 to achieve a minimum of distortion.

MATERIALS

Needle: #18 tapestry type.

Canvas: Two pieces of 12 mono mesh, each 18 by 24 inches.

Pattern: Use a commercial vest pattern in your size, or make a pattern from a vest in your wardrobe.

Persian yarn: For the vest shown, you will need the following colors and amounts. *Dark blue*—90 yards or 1½ ounces. *Medium blue*—90 yards or 1½ ounces. *Light blue*—30 yards or ½ ounce. *Green*—30 yards or ½ ounce. *Yellow*—15 yards or ¼ ounce. *Pink*—10 yards or ¼ ounce. *White*—320 yards or 5½ ounces.

GETTING STARTED

Place the left front of your vest pattern on *top* of one piece of your canvas. Holding both very straight and rigid, carefully trace the vest outline with a #2 pencil or guaranteed permanent marking pen. Do the same for the right side of your vest, and then place your canvas, with its vest shape outlined, over your design and trace. The flowers are free-flowing and can be placed at random within the vest outline.

If you would like both sides of your vest to be symmetrical, so the flowers that nod in one direction on the right side of your vest will nod

A graph of the vest pattern

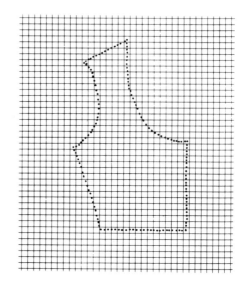

138

in the other on the left side, proceed as follows. Instead of tracing your flower design directly on to your mesh, trace it first on tracing paper with a heavy Magic Marker, so that you can see the design on *both* sides of the tracing paper. Now place your canvas over one side of the tracing and copy one side of your vest; then copy the reverse side of the tracing onto the other side of your vest.

The yarn amounts given are for the vest shown in Color Plate 13. If you would like more flowers, you may need to purchase more of the colored yarns and somewhat less of the background white. Refer to the photograph for color placement as well, although it is not a bit important that colors be used exactly as shown.

Now work the entire vest in Basketweave, using 2-ply strands of yarn.

FINISHING

Before cutting off any raw canvas, block the two pieces carefully (several times if necessary). Have the needlepoint and back section put together by an experienced seamstress to be sure of a correct fit. The lining may be silk, rayon, or satin. (See the "Blocking and Finishing" chapter for lining instructions.) The back fabric might be a matching Ottoman silk, velvet, or even felt. I have been asked why I did not needlepoint the back portion of the vest. I have found that a vest becomes too heavy when this is done, although it looks quite lovely. Sew three frog fasteners on the front.

A man's vest looks very effective trimmed in leather, with a leather, wool, or felt back. The lining might be a matching rayon or synthetic, and the closures can be small buckles, snaps, or buttons and buttonholes placed in the leather trim.

Working on Blank Canvas

Why work on blank canvas when there are so many beautiful canvases around—either painted or graphed—and you have no special artistic talent? One reason is that working on blank canvas allows you to express your own creativity through your choice of color and stitches and your placement of these two elements on the canvas. Working on blank canvas also requires no great outlay of money—only you and your needle, yarn, and canvas.

Enormous satisfaction can be found in the combination of planning and spontaneity that goes into this form of needlepoint, as well as in the total originality of the finished product.

You may want to plan your design concept in advance, working out a tentative placement of stitches and colors, or you may prefer simply to plunge in and "paint" with your yarns as you go along. I generally work out a combination of these techniques—planning consciously or unconsciously in my mind for days and sometimes weeks before reaching for that needle, yarn, and canvas and stitching away in reckless abandon. I have thought it out. I know what I want to do. Now it remains for me to see if I can create a modern artwork with the yarn as my paint and the stitches forming the brushwork.

Rainbow Wallhanging

COLOR PLATE 10

This piece is the most fun of all to work and is spectacular when completed. You will never get bored because you will never use exactly the same stitch pattern—or the same color—twice! Each square is worked differently and in a different color—132 in all! I could not always get the colors to melt into each other as I wanted them to, but the total effect was stunning anyway. I used every stitch described in this book, including each possible variation and combination thereof that I could imagine. Much of the fun lies in inventing your own variations and combinations.

MATERIALS

Needle: #18 tapestry type.

Canvas: 1 yard 10 mono mesh, 36 inches wide. The finished size is 24 by 22 inches.

Persian yarn: 20 yards or ½ ounce of each of 132 colors. Each of the eleven rows has twelve squares that fall into this general color pattern. *Row 1*—purple-reds. *Row 2*—clear reds. *Row 3*—red-oranges. *Row 4*—clear oranges. *Row 5*—orange-yellows. *Row 6*—clear yellows. *Row 7*—yellow-greens. *Row 8*—clear greens. *Row 9*—green-blues. *Row 10*—clear blues. *Row 11*—blue-purples.

I used a melange of yarns from different companies, but to make it easier for the reader I have selected color groupings from Paternayan Bros., Inc. These are Paterna Persian yarns, numbered as follows: *Row 1*—168,898,620,897, 618,615,893,612,891,205,610,105. *Row 2*—014,837,831,229,828,827, 821,232,231,236,227,221. *Row 3*—870,865,860,282,288,855,R70, 850,R60,R50,845,810. *Row 4*—464, 271,853,444,852,978,434,843,424, 968,958,242. *Row 5*—005,438,437, 467,457,442,441,447,440,427,416, 414. *Row 6*—468,458,456,580,452, 450,446,565,550,545,553,540. *Row 7*—575,570,G74,574,555,G64,G54,

(continued on next page)

GETTING STARTED

First arrange your small bundles of color in order. You may want to label them as to placement and row because many differ only slightly. However, if the colors are really close, it doesn't matter too much where you use them. Set out your yarn in eleven rows of twelve colors each. It is quite a vivid sight. Place a rubber band around each row of colors, and you are ready to begin.

Start at the upper left with your palest mauve. Use any stitch—go right through the book—and cover an area of twenty-four by twenty-four meshes for each square. This will give you a finished size of about 24 by 22 inches. If you wish to have a slightly larger wallhanging, make each square thirty by thirty meshes. I have allowed for ample yarn either way. The larger size will measure about 30 by 27½ inches.

Try for as much variety as possible in your placement of stitches. Do not, for instance, place the Diamond Eye stitch next to the Algerian Eye. For greater effect, use the Basketweave or Continental to border high-textured stitches.

Use a full 3-ply strand of Persian yarn for most of your decorative stitches, the notable exceptions being the "eye" stitches which use only a single ply, and the Basketweave or Continental which use 2-ply strands.

In the color photograph of a detail of the Rainbow Wallhanging (Color Plate 11), I have used the stitches in the following order:

Reds—Smyrna Double-Cross; Cross-Boxes in varying sizes; Rice stitch variation combining French Knots and exposed mesh; Double-Cross variation.

Oranges—Pulled-Thread stitch; Greek stitch over four meshes; Double and Tie; large and small Feather stitch variations.

Clear yellows—Sheaf variation with Smyrna Double-Cross; Knitting stitch; Weaving stitch; wide Feather stitch variation.

510,520,505,504,506. *Row 8*—592, 566,536,589,579,534,569,526,559, 524,528,340. *Row 9*—396,758, 748,765,738,728,718,783,773,763, 742,740. *Row 10*—B43,781,395, 386,754,368,385,752,330,334,365, 321. *Row 11*—012,011,641,660, 631,127,652,650,621,611,642,640.

Yellow-greens—Feather and Smyrna Double-Cross variation; group of varying size Cross stitches; Upright Cross stitch; Greek stitch over two meshes.

Greens—Rice stitch; Sheaf stitch and Diamond Eye variation; Cross-Box stitch; Scotch stitch worked to form a spiral.

Here are twelve of the stitches.

FINISHING

I did not dare attempt to frame this myself, although I do think it would look fine wrapped around a piece of plywood as described in the "Blocking and Finishing" chapter. But in this case I blocked it and then, knowing exactly what I wanted, took it to a custom framer who did a fine job following my specifications. The frame is flat white pine with a clear varnish finish, 5½ inches wide and ¾ of an inch thick. The soft natural wood tone sets off the rainbow hues without being intrusive.

Plate 1

Plate 1 **Harper's Lady**
       painted canvas

Plate 2 **Harper's Lady**

Plate 3 **On the Town**

Plate 2

Plate 3

Plate 4

Plate 5

Plate 4 **A Child's Sketch**

Plate 5 **A Child's Original Sketch**

Plate 6 **Bette Midler Record Cover**

Plate 7 **A Portrait**

Plate 8 **Floral Fabric Pillow**

Plate 9 **Greenhouse**

Plate 7

Plate 8

Plate 9

Plate 10

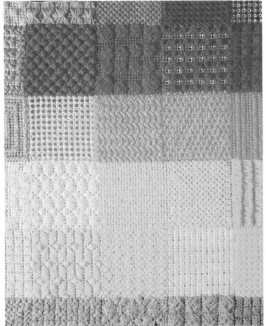

Plate 11

Plate 10 **Rainbow Wallhanging**

Plate 11 **Detail of Rainbow Wallhanging**

Plate 12

Plate 13

Plate 14

Plate 15

Plate 12 **Wallpaper motif for vest**

Plate 13 **Vest and Skirt Border**

Plate 14 **Tic-Tac-Toe Doorstop**

Plate 15 **Child's Director's Chairs**

Plate 16

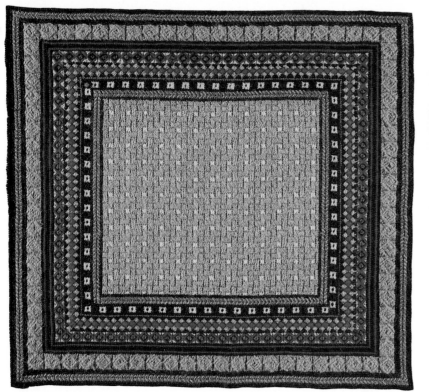

Plate 17

Plate 18

Plate 16 **Irish Village Pillow**
Plate 17 **Geometric Sampler**
Plate 18 **Detail of Geometric Sampler**

Plate 19

Plate 20

Plate 19 **Firecracker Bolster**
Plate 20 **Decorative Panel**
Plate 21 **Floral Rug**

Plate 21

Plate 22

Plate 22 **Indian Rug**
Plate 23 **Alphabet Pillows**

Plate 23

Irish Village Pillow

This lovely pillow is worked with rug yarn on quickpoint mesh in a solid white or off-white. It can also be done in any color or variety of colors. When worked on a smaller mesh the effect is delicate and lovely.

The Irish Village Pillow can be made using any combination of stitches in a succession of frames. Maximum effect is achieved when textures and shapes of juxtaposed frames are varied. Every frame can be a different stitch, or, as with the pillow described here, ten frames may use and re-use only five different stitches.

This pillow can be worked in a single day, and yet it is one of the most admired designs of all!

MATERIALS

Needle: #13 tapestry type or a blunt-pointed knitter's needle.

Canvas: ½ yard of 5 rug mesh, either mono or Penelope. The finished size is 15 by 15 inches.

Rug yarn: 350 yards or 10 ounces are required to work this pillow. Add another 132 yards or 4 ounces if you want four nice thick tassels at the corners.

A small Smyrna Double-Cross variation

The Feather variation

GETTING STARTED

Cut your mesh to a piece 18 by 18 inches, then fold it in half horizontally and vertically to find the approximate center. It is not important to be absolutely accurate. In the center where your folds met, with your canvas opened flat again, work a Smyrna Double-Cross variation over only two canvas threads. Work three more Smyrna Double-Cross stitches to the right and three to the left of this first one. This will form the center row of seven rows of Smyrna. In other words, having completed your first row, you will now work three similar rows above it and three more below it.

Now begin to work your frames around this central portion. Your stitches will keep changing direction on each side of your frame. Begin at the lower right-hand corner of the center square; working upward along the right side of the square, work a variation of the Feather stitch (see the illustrations below and on page 144) with each diagonal reaching up three meshes and over two. For a special effect here, begin immediately with your first full-length stitch. Later on, instead of compensating, you will use Continental stitches to fill in the canvas left exposed at the corners.

Whenever you work a pillow made up of ever-enlarging frames, such as this one, here is a rule to remember. The *length* of the stitch you are forming tells you how far *beyond* the previous frame you must work. You have begun this Feather stitch frame even with the lower right-hand corner of the central square. *But*, as this Feather stitch covers three meshes in length, you will work up to and beyond the upper right-hand corner by three meshes. To begin the next side of your frame, you will turn your canvas clockwise and once again start on the right even with the Smyrna stitches—and you will work beyond them by three meshes. Work the rest of the frame in the same manner.

Notice that the Feather stitch variation forms a continuous, even,

143

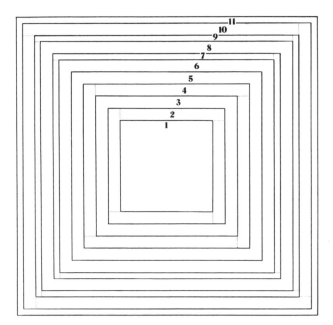

Here is how the stitches are used.

high ridge of diagonals. This is an excellent contrast in size, direction, shape, and texture to the Smyrna Double-Cross.

For the second frame, work three rows of Basketweave or Continental. While doing so, cover the exposed canvas on all four sides where the Feather stitch was not compensated.

Now begin the third frame. Work a Sheaf stitch made up of three four-mesh uprights, pinched in at the center by a stitch that covers two meshes. Fill in the uncovered space between each motif with a simple

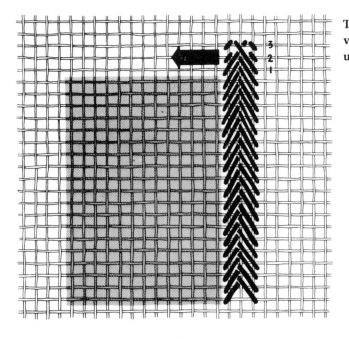

The Feather variation as it is used in a corner

144

two-mesh upright stitch. Once again you will be starting on a line even with any corner of your previous frame and will work beyond that frame. As your Sheaf stitch is four meshes long, you will now work four meshes beyond each corner.

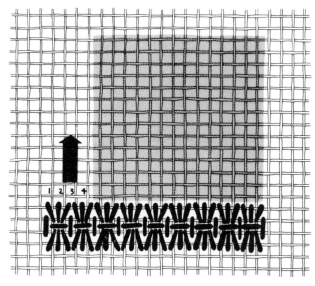

The Sheaf stitch (note how the bottom row extends four meshes beyond the previous frame).

When working the Sheaf stitch, start at the bottom right-hand corner and work toward the left along the bottom to four meshes beyond the lower left-hand corner. Then, turning the pillow counterclockwise, start again working from right to left. Continue in this manner until all four sides are completed.

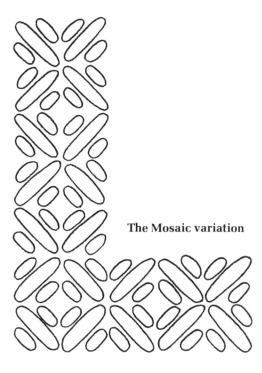

The Mosaic variation

The next two frames are worked in the Flat stitch (see the Parisian stitch, Diagrams 5 and 6). This stitch is made up of three stitches to a motif, and it covers a total of only two meshes. In the Flat stitch, the little Mosaic motifs keep changing direction. Work two frames of this stitch, reaching just two meshes beyond the corner with each frame.

As the Flat stitch keeps changing direction, there is no really comfortable way to do it. Begin at any corner. The mesh will show through a bit where the motifs meet, but this is part of the "look." If you want more texture, and object to the canvas showing, work a French Knot in each of these spaces. Now work three more rows of Basketweave all the way around.

The next frame is the slanted Gobelin, worked up and over two meshes. Compensate with a single little slanting stitch at the corners when beginning your rows and again when ending.

Your eighth frame will consist of two more rows of the Smyrna Double-Cross stitch that covers only two meshes. It will be worked two meshes beyond each corner as you work around each frame.

Frame 9 repeats the slanted Gobelin, worked up and over two meshes. Remember to compensate at the beginning and end of each row.

Frame 10 repeats the Sheaf stitch. Frame 11 consists of two more rows of Basketweave, worked around the outside edge. Much of this will be turned under when the pillow is made up.

FINISHING

Using a nice heavy wool or velvet to back this pillow, have it mounted or follow directions for mounting a knife-edged pillow in the "Blocking and Finishing" chapter.

If you would like to make tassels, fold about thirty 18-inch strands of rug yarn in half. With a 13-inch strand, tie them loosely together at the top. With another 13-inch strand, cinch the bundle with a tight knot about an inch from the top. Now take a needle and weave each of the two ends of this strand through the center of the tassel where they will not show.

Attach the tassel to the pillow by taking one end of the top 13-inch strand and sewing it through the corner of your pillow. Knot this end with the other end near your top knot. Then weave the two cut ends back into your pillow, emerging some distance from the corner and snipping off the yarn as close to the surface of the pillow as possible so it will not show.

Repeat this at all four corners. When all tassels have been attached, trim the ends so they are even with the tassel.

Here is how to make a tassel.

Geometric Sampler

COLOR PLATE 17

*This beautiful sampler, simply another form of the Irish Village
Pillow worked on smaller mesh, was color-coordinated and
executed by Mr. Per Buan. It is worked in successive frames exactly
like that pillow but uses a completely different variety of stitches.*

MATERIALS

Needle: #18 or #20 tapestry type.

Canvas: Cut a 20-by-20-inch piece
of 14 mono canvas. The finished
size is 15½ by 14½ inches.

Persian yarns: This sampler
requires a total of 450 yards or 7½
ounces, divided as follows.
Medium beige (or your primary
color)—150 yards or 2½ ounces.
Dark brown—60 yards or 1 ounce.
Rust—60 yards or 1 ounce. *Palest
beige*—60 yards or 1 ounce. *Silver
gray*—60 yards or 1 ounce. *Dark
turquoise*—60 yards or 1 ounce.

GETTING STARTED

Because the Cross-Box stitch is so difficult to compensate, I avoid the
problem by starting this pillow with that stitch. As it is placed in one
of the outer frames, I work inward, instead of vice versa. This creates
some other problems, but they are easier to deal with than attempting
either an exact canvas count or elaborate compensation. Use 2-ply
strands for all stitches except the "eye" stitches. If you feel this is too
thick, try a single ply; if it covers, use it.

Start about 7¼ inches from the raw edge of your 20-by-20-inch
canvas. Work the Cross-Box stitch over nine canvas threads. Work
twenty-two boxes along one side and twenty-one along the other. This
forms Frame 10. Several frames will be added outside of this one later,
but for now, concentrate on working in toward the center. The
Cross-Box is worked in medium beige.

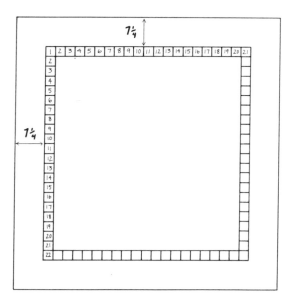

**Getting started on
your sampler**

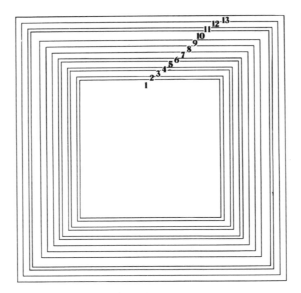

Here is a key to the sampler frames.

Frame 9 consists of six rows of Basketweave in the following colors: first and outermost row, dark brown; second row, rust; third and fourth rows, dark brown again; fifth row, rust; and sixth row, dark brown. The Basketweave here sets off the high-textured Cross-Box stitch.

Frame 8—working in toward the center—is the Flat stitch variation of the Scotch stitch in four colors: dark brown; rust; dark turquoise; and silver gray. When you feel secure with this stitch formation, you may find it easier to work one color at a time, starting with the largest stitch in rust.

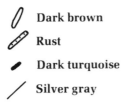

Dark brown

Rust

Dark turquoise

Silver gray

The Scotch stitch variation with its color code

The Flat stitch takes on an entirely new personality when worked in many colors. Instead of forming small boxes, it now forms large repeating diamonds. The Flat stitch is fairly easy to compensate (see Scotch stitch Diagram 9, right-hand side), but do count ahead as you approach your corners to be sure to form any necessary compensating motifs *before* you reach the corner. Your corner motifs should always be the full stitch.

Frame 7 has three full rows of the Smyrna Double-Cross stitch. The first row is medium beige, the second is rust, and the third is medium beige again, with the compensating stitches at the top and bottom worked in dark brown.

When working the first row of Smyrna, once again compensate with a slightly *abbreviated stitch before* you reach the corners, if necessary.

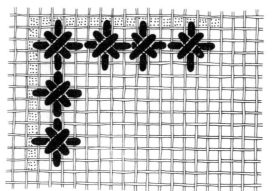

Compensate the Smyrna Double-Cross in this manner (note second stitch from the right, top row).

Frame 6 is a single row of Continental worked in brown and dark turquoise.

Frame 5 is the Algerian Eye worked with a single ply of yarn. Work one eye in silver gray and the next in dark brown. While all four corner eyes need not be the same color, once again the motif in each corner should be a complete stitch, with any necessary compensating done before you reach the corner. These should form a checkerboard effect around the frame. If you find, as you near the end, that two eyes of the same color will meet, then simply form a few compensated eyes one or two meshes narrower to allow you to fit in an extra motif.

Frame 4 is one row of the Continental stitch in brown.

Frame 3 is the Feather stitch two meshes high and a total of four meshes wide in alternating colors of medium beige and dark turquoise. The Color Plate 18 will help you visualize how this is done. Stitches sharing a hole each slant up and over two meshes and should be the same color, with each row extending all the way to the corner and beginning and ending with a little compensating stitch. I usually work down one side in one color, skipping over one hole as I go to allow for filling in with the second color on my way back up the row. It is faster that way.

Frame 2 is a row of Continental in dark brown. Frame 1 (the center area) is worked in alternating colors of medium beige and palest beige. Start in the approximate center and work out toward the sides following the graphed design.

If I were working this, I might be tempted to substitute a "disappearing" letter of the alphabet (see pages 172–84) with a background of the Scotch stitch for the graphed design. The letter could be worked in rust or dark brown, the background in alternating colors of medium beige and palest beige.

Finally, add the following frames *outside* the Cross-Box border.

This graph shows the center section of the sampler.

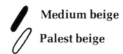

/ Medium beige

/ Palest beige

Frame 11—just around the border—will be two rows of Basketweave or Continental in dark brown.

Frame 12 will be another row of the Feather stitch worked in alternating colors of medium beige and dark turquoise as before.

Frame 13 consists of three final rows of Basketweave or Continental in dark brown. These final rows, which generally get turned under in the mounting, are important because they prevent any of the decorative stitchery from getting lost.

FINISHING

Block the piece and make it into a knife-edged pillow. The sampler could have several other possible uses as well. It might be lined in heavy silk and fitted with two ribbon ties to become a handkerchief case. It could be lined and trimmed with soft leather and folded over to form a tie case. It could be made up into a stunning tote bag. Or it could be made, as this was, into a leatherbound book cover for an heirloom album. Take your pick! Or perhaps you have still a better idea.

Working from Graphs

Why work from graphs? There are several reasons. A graphed design may be so lovely that it is irresistible; graphed designs are far less expensive than their painted counterparts; and they are the best way to preserve traditional needlepoint designs, as well as to transpose precise geometric designs. If exact reproduction is what you seek, a graph is surely the most effective way to achieve this.

Some people, I have found, are thrown off by painted canvases and prefer always to work from a graph, finding satisfaction in its precision. But is creativity or even originality possible within the context of this precision?

There are three methods by which you can put your own stamp on a graphed design. The first is borrowing elements of a graphed design and redistributing them. This is the basis of the Floral Rug design graphed on pages 160–64. The elements remain the same, but the finished product becomes your own design.

The second method utilizes color. If you change the colors of the original, you change the original itself.

The third method involves stitch selection. Here too you can experiment, using different textures within a given design.

But despite the aforementioned, most people who work from graphs do so because they wish to reproduce exactly what they have seen. To these people I would say that if you love a design, it is well worth the effort of working it. It will always give you pleasure.

151

Firecracker Bolster

This lively bolster pillow can be worked up in a day or two. It makes a great addition to a student's college room, an imaginative gift for a new baby, or an explosive present for anyone with a spark.

MATERIALS

Needle: # 13 quickpoint tapestry type or a blunt-ended knitter's needle.

Canvas: Cut a 2-by-24-inch piece of 5 mesh, mono or Penelope. The finished size is 18 by 20 inches.

Rug yarn: You will need a total of 280 yards or 17 ounces. You may, if desired, substitute two full strands of Persian yarn for each strand of rug yarn. If this does not cover properly, add a few more plies. *Royal blue*—74 yards or 4½ ounces. *Crimson*—74 yards of 4½ ounces. *White*—132 yards or 8 ounces.

GETTING STARTED

With a pencil, draw your outside measurements of 18 inches long by 20 inches wide on your quickpoint mesh. Plot out the name, nickname, or initials (no more than six letters in all) in plain block letters on graph paper. You will only need to graph the consonants as I have already graphed the "firecracker" vowels for you to follow. Each consonant should be sixteen meshes high. They need not be—and usually are not—equally wide. As you have a width of about sixty meshes on which to fit the lettering, the maximum width of any single letter should be about eight meshes. One or two letters might use more mesh if other letters use less, or if you use fewer letters. Allow at least two meshes between each letter. The entire name should extend about 11 –12 inches across, with the same number of meshes on either side of the lettering.

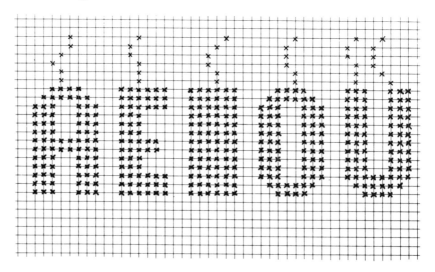

The firecracker vowels

152

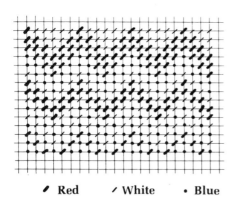

✎ Red   ✎ White   • Blue

The lightning design and legend

About midway up your mesh, center the letters, using a small single-mesh Diagonal Cross stitch in the blue rug yarn. Then place a frame (see Color Plate 19) around the letters in a position about six meshes from the end of your lettering at either side, and four meshes from the tops and bottoms of your letters. With the blue yarn, work this as before in a small Diagonal Cross stitch over one mesh.

The background should be filled with white around the letters and inside the frame. Use a larger Diagonal Cross stitch over two meshes. Work the balance of the pillow in Basketweave and Continental, using random waves of crimson, blue, and white. Follow the graph for this lightning design.

FINISHING

Block the piece well. Trim to ¾ of an inch and turn under the side edges, then, along each edge, sew a piece of gay matching fabric folded in half to measure 12 inches wide. The folded edge will be the outer edge. Turn the raw mesh under at top and bottom, and blind-sew the needlepoint together to form a roll. Fill the center portion of this roll with a foam bolster form that is 20 inches long and 19–20 inches in circumference. Center the bolster form, and tie both ends (around the fabric and up against the form) with colorful matching bows of ribbon about 4 inches wide.

Decorative Panel

The vivid colors of this panel give it a South American feeling, and in fact it was adapted from some wallpaper (see the "Shopping Guide"), which was in turn adapted from an old Peruvian vest. I loved it so much that I simply could not decide which of the many possible ideas for its use appealed to me the most. Originally, I had planned to use it as a vertical panel to be worn over a long gray flannel evening skirt. It was to attach to a needlepoint belt that had some of the same design and colors, and would hang loosely down the front of the skirt. But then, when it was completed, it occurred to me how beautiful it would look hanging on the wall, upholstered down the center of a precious armchair, draped over a window as a valance, or, as shown in Color Plate 20, gracing the center of a lovely old table.

Perhaps you will find yet another use for this beautiful piece.

The Decorative Panel used as an apron

MATERIALS

Needle: #18 tapestry type.

Canvas: 1⅓ yards of 12 mono canvas. The finished size is about 37¼ by 8¼ inches. Cut the piece 42 by 13 inches.

Persian yarn: You will need a total of about 750 yards or 12½ ounces of yarn. This is a generous estimate as there is quite a bit of waste. The amounts given below are sufficient to work a panel the size of mine. Should you wish to work another size, allow 2½ yards to the square inch to find your total requirements, and then use the percentage of each color that I have listed below. (See "Questions and Answers: Needles and Yarn" for computing the number of ounces you might need.) Use full 3-ply strands. *White*—(Paterna #005) 150 yards or 2½ ounces, or 20 percent. *Orange*—(Paterna #970) 188 yards or 3¼ ounces, or 25 percent. *Green*—(Paterna #G64) 112 yards or 2 ounces, or 15 percent. *Fuchsia*—(Paterna #649) 75 yards or 1¼ ounces, or 10 percent. *Black*—(Paterna #050) 75

(continued on page 156)

GETTING STARTED

Work the entire length of the panel from top to bottom, one color at a time. Start at the right side and work toward the left. Follow the graph on page 155 carefully, noting which color and which stitch to use in each area.

Row A is worked in the Greek stitch in green over two meshes. If you have never done the Greek stitch, practice it as shown on pages 65–67 over three mesh before attempting the two-mesh variation in Diagram 7. Row B is worked in the same stitch with fuchsia yarn. The letter C on the graph indicates a row of triangles. These move down the line in *pairs* of identical colors that are outlined in black, orange, and white. Only the center portion of each pair changes color as follows—from top to bottom: fuchsia, green, blue, crimson, then repeat. The graph indicates the second of the fuchsia pairs, followed by a pair of green triangles, which in turn is followed by two blue triangles, and so on. Color Plate 20 should help you to visualize this sequence.

When the central portion is completed, work the left border in the same manner as the right. After blocking, use a binding stitch (in white yarn) that covers two meshes around the outside border.

FINISHING

Steam press the edges back, and line the piece with a coordinating fabric. Directions for lining are given in the "Blocking and Finishing"

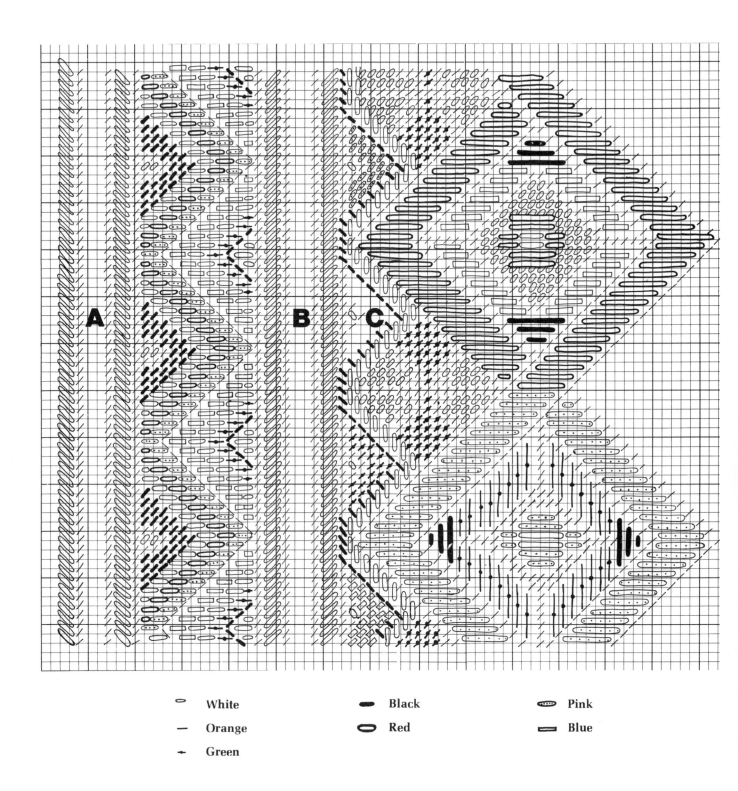

⊝	White	⬛	Black	⬭	Pink
—	Orange	⬭	Red	⬓	Blue
↤	Green				

A graph and color key. The size and direction of each stitch is shown in the graph.

yards or 1¼ ounces, or 10 percent.
Crimson—(Paterna #958) 75 yards
or 1¼ ounces, or 10 percent.
Blue—(Paterna #752) 75 yards or
1¼ ounces, or 10 percent.

I have specified the Paterna Persian
colors because so much of the
dazzling effect of this panel is due
to the juxtaposition of hot colors. If
you prefer a softer look, substitute
colors at will.

chapter. This pattern can, of course, be adapted to make pillows, a
stunning vest, or even a rug! If I wished to use this pattern for a project
that called for more width, I would center the large diamonds and
repeat another row of them on either side, retaining the thin lines
running vertically on either side. Only at the far edges of my design
would I add back the pairs of small triangles. If I were working a vest, I
might first work the small triangle pairs *horizontally* along the bottom
edge and vertically where the two sides of the vest meet, then work the
rest of the vest in the vertical large diamonds only. As I describe it, it
sounds so lovely that I believe I shall get to work on just such a vest!

Floral Rug

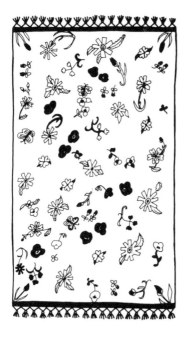

This gorgeous rug is designed with a lady bug, a butterfly, and eleven different flowers, in varying colors, scattered at random over a soft green background. Each type of flower usually reappears in the same colors, but the butterfly keeps changing its hue. You may decide to work it in your own way, but the basic idea is to make this rug your own by placing the graphed flowers wherever you choose. There is no special reason for these being where they are, nor is there any special reason for the background being green. It could just as well be a soft blue, jet black, deep brown, bright coral, old rose, or any other color you like. Just remember that your other colors must have adequate contrast to show up properly.

MATERIALS

Needle: #18 tapestry type.

Canvas: 2 yards of 36-inch-wide 10 mono canvas. You can substitute Penelope canvas for the mono if you wish to work parts of the flowers or butterflies in petit-point. The finished size is about 33 by 57 inches.

Persian yarn: The total required is about 4,800 yards or 5 pounds. The following amounts are approximations only, based on the rug shown in Color Plate 21. As you may wish to change the colors, I am listing the percentage of the total beside each color to help you with your calculations.
Primary colors: *Red*—240 yards or 4 ounces, or 5 percent.
Yellow—240 yards or 4 ounces, or

(continued on next page)

GETTING STARTED

Pencil in the outline of your rug—33 inches wide by 57 inches long. Now study the graphed flowers on pages 159–64 and visualize them on the surface of your canvas. You can tell how large each one is by counting the meshes covered. Every ten meshes equals an inch. You might then pencil on your mesh a number where each flower will go. Start anywhere. If you want to superimpose some flowers, complete the forwardmost flower first, and then place a portion of another peeking out from behind it.

Your background can be worked last or filled in around the flowers as they are completed. You will be using full 3-ply strands of your Persian yarns on the 10 mesh, and it is most important that you work in Basketweave wherever possible (or the special form of the Continental described on pages 39–40) to avoid massive distortion. On a large project such as this, you might want to use a floor frame. This will slow you down considerably, but it will keep your work free of distortion. Needlepoint canvas is never absolutely straight, but if a large piece such as this gets pulled too badly out of shape, even repeated blockings may fail to achieve acceptable results.

5 percent. *Dark green*—240 yards or 4 ounces, or 5 percent. *Light green*—240 yards or 4 ounces, or 5 percent.
Secondary colors: *Dark pink*—216 yards or 3¾ ounces, or 4½ percent. *Light pink*—144 yards or 2½ ounces, or 3 percent. *Purple*—120 yards or 2 ounces, or 2½ percent. *Light orange*—96 yards or 1¾ ounces, or 2 percent.
Tertiary colors: *Dark rose*—72 yards or 1¼ ounces, or 1½ percent. *Light rose*—72 yards or 1¼ ounces, or 1½ percent. *Dark orange*—72 yards or 1¼ ounces, or 1½ percent. *Blue*—48 yards or 1 ounce, or 1 percent. *Dark plum*—48 yards or 1 ounce, or 1 percent.
Accent colors: *Dark blue*—24 yards or ½ ounce, or ½ percent. *Mauve*—24 yards or ½ ounce, or ½ percent. *Dark aqua*—24 yards or ½ ounce, or ½ percent.
Background: *Palest green*—2,880 yards or 3 pounds, or 60 percent.

You may decide to do the entire rug in black and white and shades of gray, or work it entirely in blues. Pick your own colors. Arrange the flowers in your own way rather than as you see them here. You might place them all in one corner, or scattered more profusely one behind another. Turn them upside down or sideways. But remember —the graphs are only to give you a start; the finished rug will be your own design.

FINISHING

This rug can be used on the floor—yes, and walked on—or hung on the wall. If you do not wish it to get too much wear but would like to use it on the floor, place it under a glass-topped coffee table in front of a sofa, where it can be seen but not stepped on. Or use it beside your bed where mostly bare feet will tread on it.

Line the back of the rug—or wallhanging—with canvas or heavy linen in two pieces to form a flap, as shown in the illustration below. Further instructions on lining needlepoint can be found in the "Blocking and Finishing" chapter. A heavy matching fringe can then be machine sewn along the two short ends.

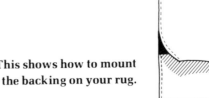

This shows how to mount the backing on your rug.

Graphed flowers

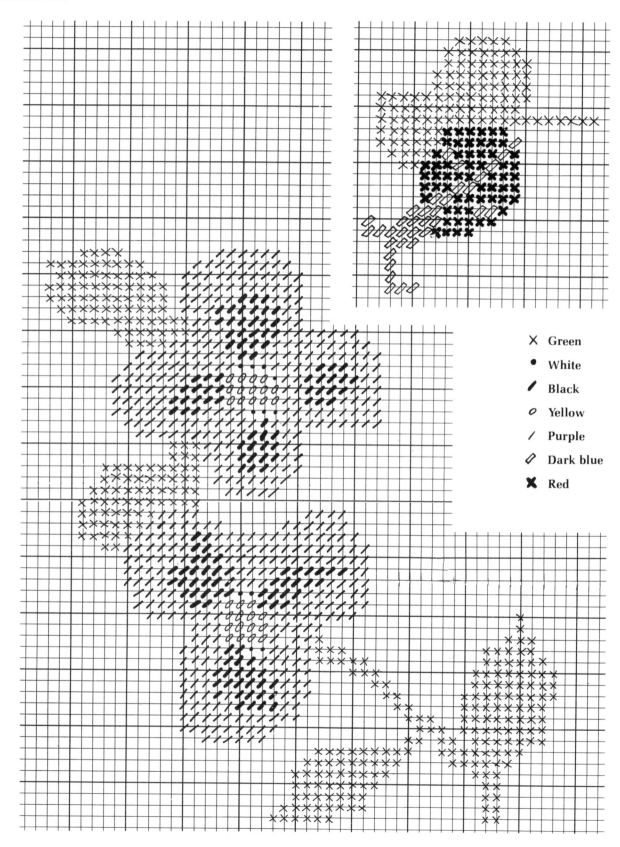

X Green

● White

／ Black

O Yellow

／ Purple

◇ Dark blue

✖ Red

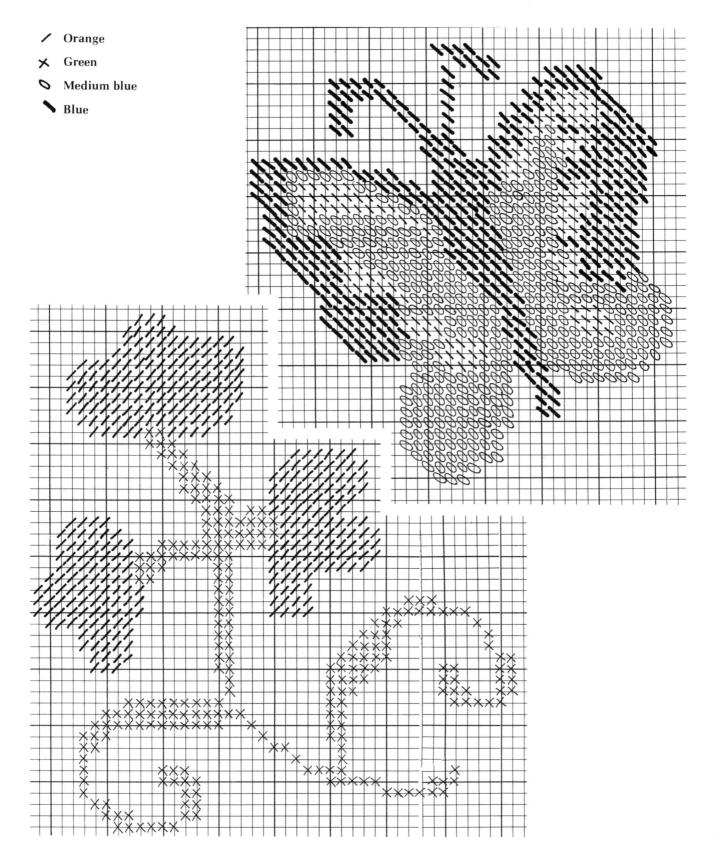

/ Orange

✗ Green

∂ Medium blue

＼ Blue

160

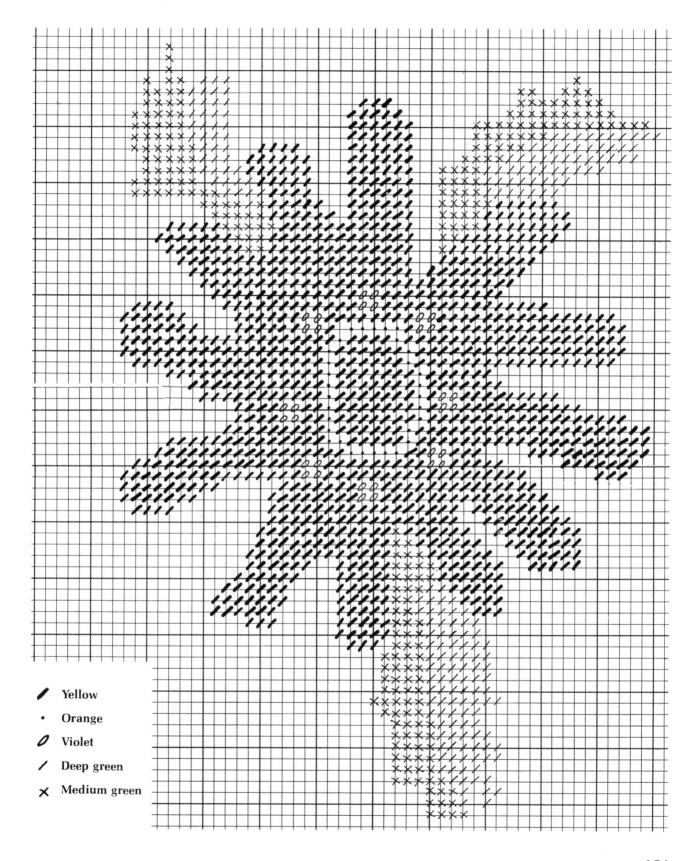

/ Yellow

• Orange

0 Violet

/ Deep green

✗ Medium green

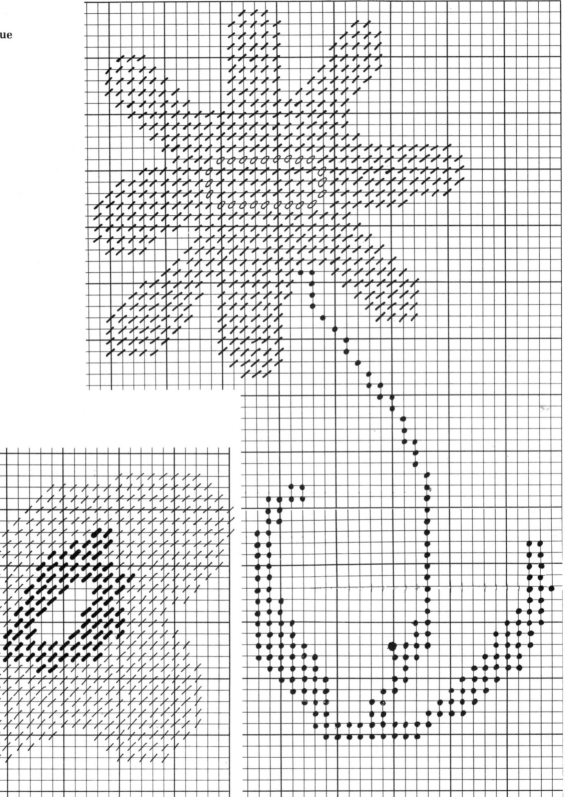

Red

Navy blue

Orange

Yellow

Green

/ Pink
• Deep pink
/ Green
○ Navy blue
✕ Red or Orange
◇ Light blue

163

- ● Rose
- ✕ Deep pink
- / Green

Skirt Border

When fashion suddenly decreed that skirt lengths fall dramatically, my daughter literally got "caught short." She had enjoyed wearing her lovely brown velvet skirt with a matching vest for less than a year, and now it was some 3 inches too short! Needlepoint came to the rescue.

This type of border can also be used to enhance the bottom of a long evening skirt. For an extra-wide border, I can visualize this pattern worked twice, one motif on top of the other, so it forms two rows of interlocking design. The outer border could then be worked around these. Color Plate 13 might help you envision this possibility.

This design has a width of 3¼ inches on 14 mesh. If your skirt needs more length than this, or if you wish a wider border for any reason, you might work the design on a 12 mesh or simply extend the area around the central motif as much as needed before adding back the borders. Conversely, a 16 or 18 mesh could be used for a narrower width.

The circumference of this skirt was 63 inches, but as yours is sure to be different, I shall give yarn amounts according to the number of motifs (each one measures 2¼ inches on 14 mesh) you will be working.

MATERIALS

Needle: #18 tapestry type.

Canvas: For my skirt border I used a piece of 14 mono canvas 8 by 67 inches. The finished size was 3¼ by 63 inches. (If you add 4 inches to your width measure and 4 inches to your length measure, you will have enough canvas.)

Persian yarn: I used a total of about 350 yards or 6 ounces. One complete motif (2¼ inches) requires the following colors and amounts. *Lightest beige*—4 yards. *Rust*—2¾ yards. *Medium beige*—1⅓ yards. *Darkest brown*—2¾ yards. *Café au lait*—1½ yards

If you are buying your yarn by the ounce, figure out how many motifs you will be working, add up your total yard requirements, and check the conversion table in the "Questions and Answers" section on page 4.

GETTING STARTED

Working with a 2-ply strand of Persian yarn, follow the graph on page 166. Start in the center of your canvas and work toward the outer edges, first in one direction and then in the other. This way, when the two ends are joined, even if they do not form a complete motif (mine worked out perfectly to half a motif on each end), it will not show too much.

You might want to keep two needles threaded, one with rust and the other with dark brown. When you have temporarily finished with one color, let the leftover yarn dangle in *front* of your work somewhere outside the border (keeping an eye on it until you need it again so it does not become tangled in your subsequent stitches), and then pick up the other color.

Following the graph, work the rust motif until it meets the dark brown. Now work the dark brown until it meets the rust, and then reverse the procedure. If you attempt to work all of one color before starting on the next, a mistake early on can keep you ripping for hours!

When all the motifs are completed, work the area inside your rust-and-brown chain design. The numbers on the graph represent the size of each stitch. For example, a number 4 means that stitch will cover

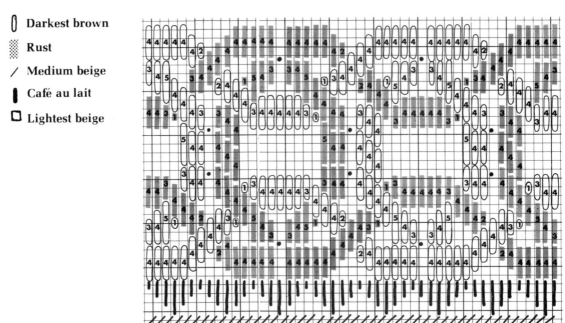

The graph and color key
for the Skirt Border

four canvas threads. A dot in the background area indicates the size limit of a stitch. Where no dot appears, one stitch fills the entire blank area.

As you work your background from one area to the next, pull your leftover yarn across the back and weave it in and out of the stitches in the direction toward which you are moving.

Remember, try not to work one whole motif at one far end and a partial motif at the other, as the joining will look awkward. Rather work two partial motifs and join them along the side or back seam of your skirt.

After completing the inside of your chain motifs, work the café au lait outermost border in a slanting Gobelin stitch, top and bottom. Finally work the two-tone design around the outside of the motifs.

FINISHING

Once finished, I blocked my border and brought it to a dressmaker because my sewing skills are dismal. It is possible to sew on your own border by cutting the edges of raw canvas to about ¾ of an inch, pressing these back with a steam iron, then sewing a lining of silk or dress-weight rayon in a matching brown on the reverse side. This lined border is then blind-stitched to the bottom of your skirt. The border is superimposed directly on top of the skirt material in the case of a long evening skirt, and the ends are joined at the side or back seam. For further instructions, see the "Blocking and Finishing" chapter.

Indian Rug

This beautiful rug, an adaptation of an old Indian design, is being worked by Mr. Per Buan. It is about half finished now, but by the time this book is published it should be complete. It is worked in Basketweave in only seven colors with full 3-ply strands of Persian yarn. It is simple, quick to do, and a joy to behold.

It is important to work this in Basketweave or the special form of the Continental described on pages 39–40 or on a floor frame. Although needlepoint will never be exactly straight, working a large piece such as this in the regular Continental stitch would pull it so badly out of shape that no amount of blocking could restore it. A frame will hold it securely in shape but will slow you down considerably. To my mind, this rug is not large enough to make a frame necessary, but if I were working a room-sized rug I would use a frame to ensure the absolute minimum of canvas distortion.

MATERIALS

Needle: #18 tapestry type.

Canvas: 2½ yards of 10 mono canvas, 36 inches wide. The finished size is 35 by 72 inches.

Persian yarn: You will need a total of about 5,760 yards or 6 pounds. (Each single row of needlepoint, from right to left, requires 9 yards of yarn.) *Blue*—1,800 yards or 30 ounces. *Purple-red*—1,000 yards or 17 ounces. *Green*—240 yards or 4 ounces. *Black*—700 yards or 12 ounces. *Brown*—36 yards or ¾ ounce. *Soft pink*—450 yards or 7½ ounces. *Beige* (background) —1,500 yards or 25 ounces.

GETTING STARTED

Leave a full 2 inches of raw canvas before beginning to work at the top, following the graphed design on pages 168–69. The graph depicts one half of the length of the completed rug and only a portion of the width, which will measure 35 inches when finished. Therefore, continue each row to a width of 35 inches. Note that, as in all Indian rugs, individual design motifs—whether zigzags or diamonds—are never identical, and they need not end symmetrically at the far sides.

When you have reached the bottom of the graph, repeat the design in mirror image so all the diamonds are in the center and the broad bands reach out to the ends. The Color Plate 22 will help you visualize the end result.

167

- •   Blue
- ❬   Black
- ╱   Green
- ╲   Beige
- ●   Purple/Red
- ✕   Soft Pink
- O   Brown

FINISHING

Block the rug as often as necessary to get it back into shape. It may never hang exactly straight, but do the best you can. A fringe looks lovely sewn on the short ends.

Turn the long sides under, steam press, and back the rug with burlap, canvas, or heavy linen in two pieces as shown in the illustration on page 158. If the rug is to be used on the floor, a good trick is to sew rubber sealer rings from mason jars on the back of the four corners to keep it from slipping on a bare floor. For further instructions about lining needlepoint, consult the "Blocking and Finishing" chapter.

Alphabet Pillow

These disappearing letters are quite amazing. If you look at them from the proper angle they are crystal-clear. But as your angle of vision changes, the letters maddeningly disappear and become nothing more than abstract forms that are impossible to decipher.

Once you have "uncovered" the letters, you can usually find them again. But if they cause you too much frustration, just use yarn to fill in the dotted lines shown on the graphs. The letters will no longer disappear and you will still have a handsome, graphic letter form. However, if you enjoy the disappearing act as I do, then do not fill in the dotted lines when following the graphs.

My letters were worked in black yarn on 12 mesh. On one little pillow, I chose not to fill in the background, but left the canvas exposed. I had this pillow mounted with a gingham flounce. On my other alphabet pillow, I sought a more modern look, so I worked the background as well as the letter in Basketweave, and then finished it with a piped knife-edge.

On a 12 mesh, each letter is about 4 inches high. You can make them bigger or smaller by changing your mesh size. You can even work them in quickpoint on a 5 mesh. This alphabet can be used to form words, sayings, full names, or just initials. It can be worked in color, and the background can be left blank or filled in. The pillows are marvelous looking, completely tantalizing and can be finished in a jiffy!

MATERIALS

Needle: #18 tapestry type.

Canvas: A 12-by-12-inch piece of 12 mono canvas. The finished size is 8 by 8 inches without the flounce.

Persian yarn: You may work another size, but my flounced pillow used these amounts. *Black*—20 yards or ½ ounce for each letter. If you fill in the background, you will need 115 yards or 1¾ ounces.

GETTING STARTED

Begin at the upper right-hand corner of your letter graph, about 2 inches up and to the right of where you wish to place the center of your letter. On 12 mesh you will use only a 2-ply strand of Persian yarn if you work your letter in Basketweave or Continental. If you wish to use a decorative stitch, you will probably need a full 3-ply strand of yarn.

Do *not* work the stitches that appear as dotted lines on the graphs if you want the letters to disappear. Working the dotted stitches will form a letter that will always be visible.

FINISHING

If you have used Basketweave or almost any decorative stitch to form your letters and have not filled in the background, blocking will probably be unnecessary. If you have filled in the background, then it is best to block the canvas to give the work a smooth and even appearance. See the "Blocking and Finishing" chapter if you wish to mount this little pillow yourself.

171

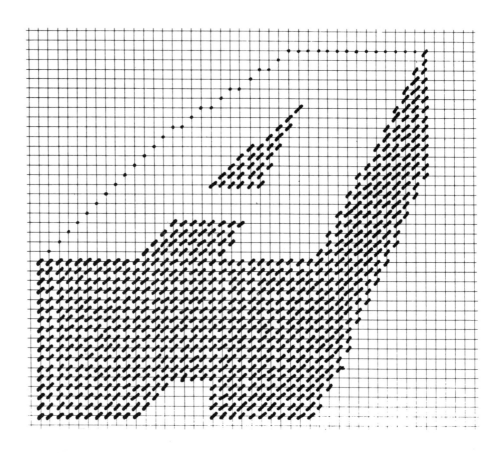

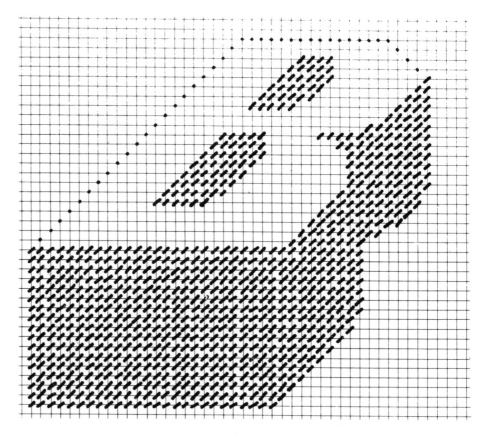

172

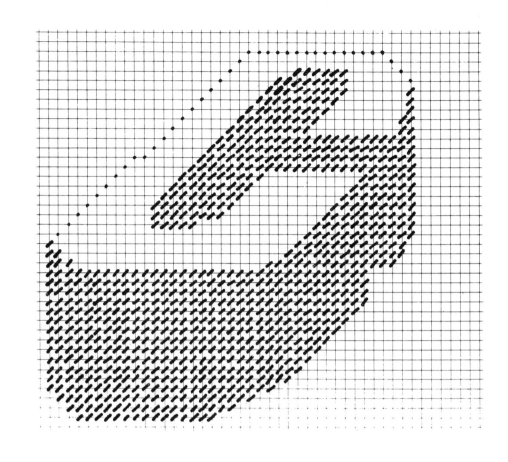

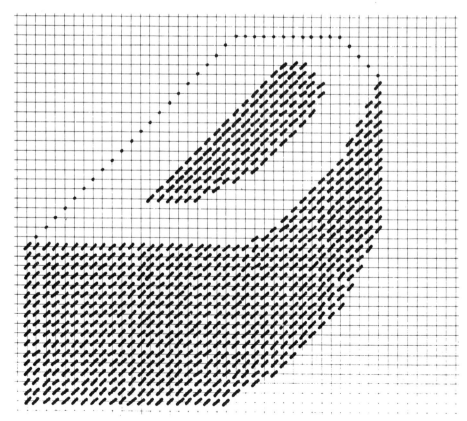

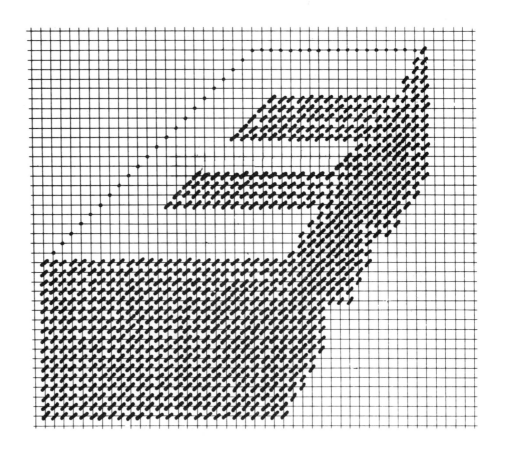

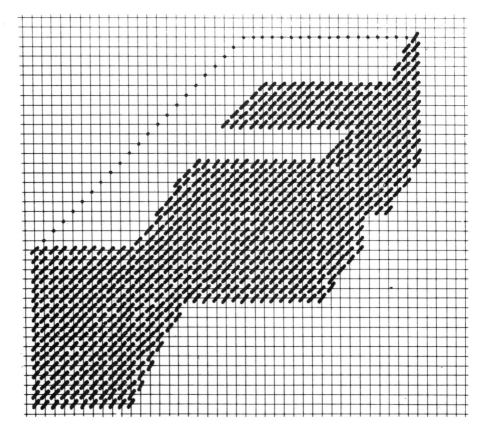

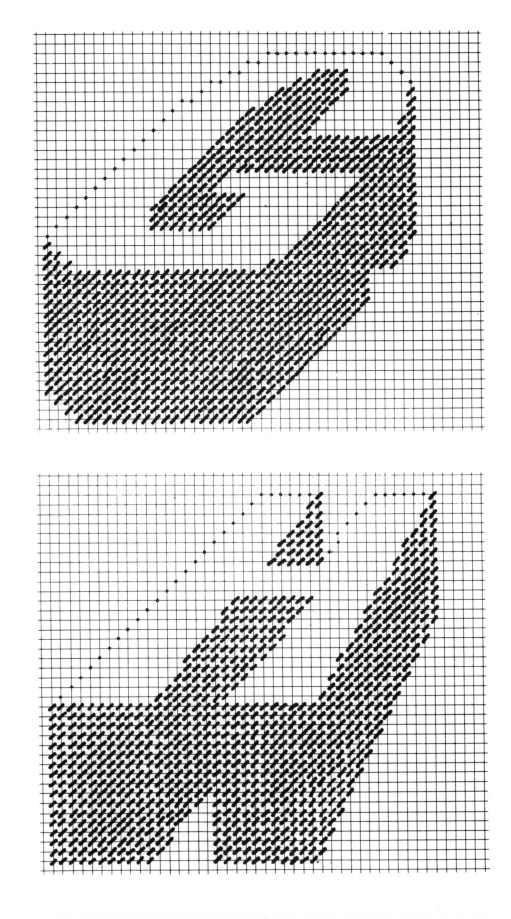

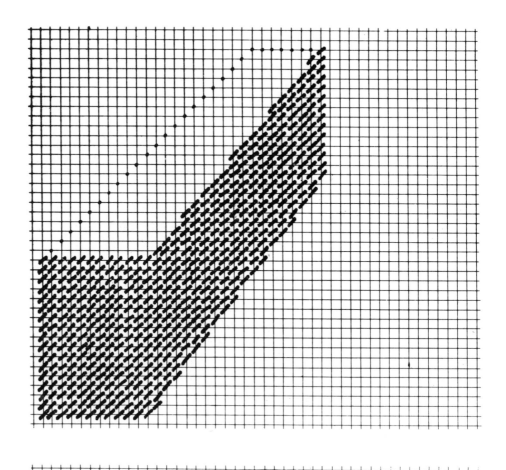

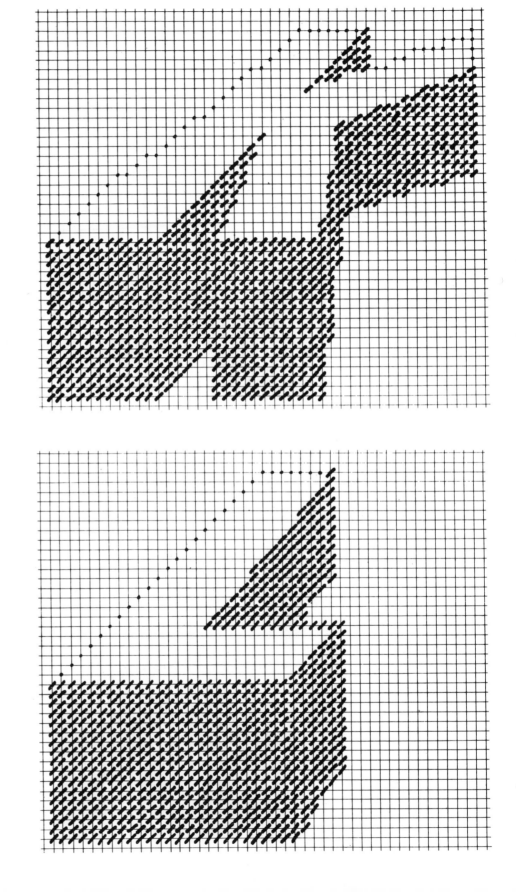

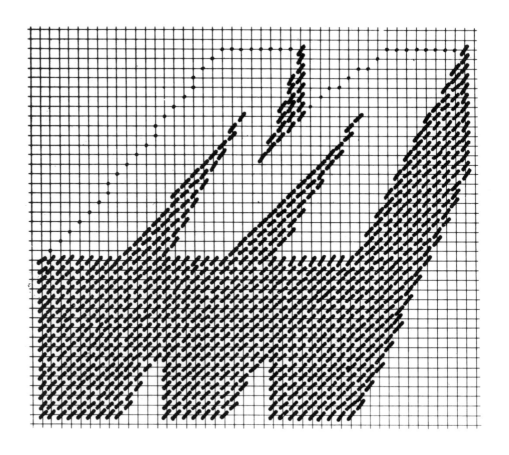

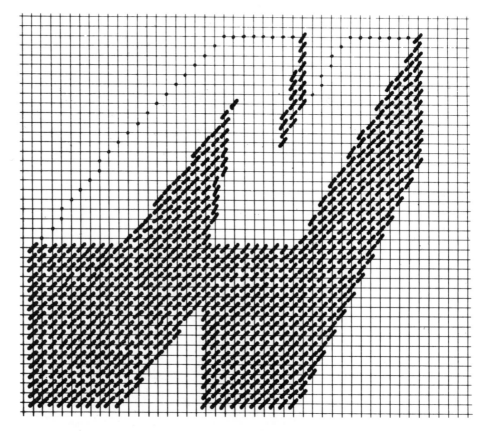

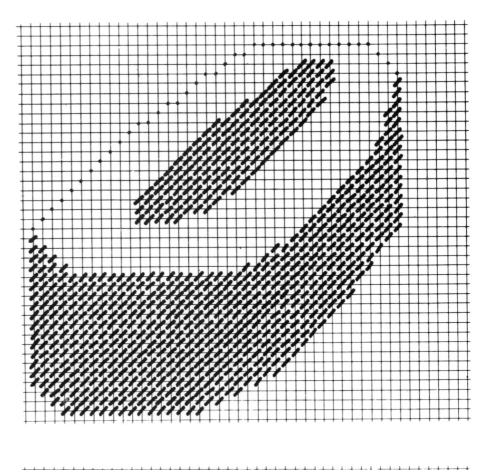

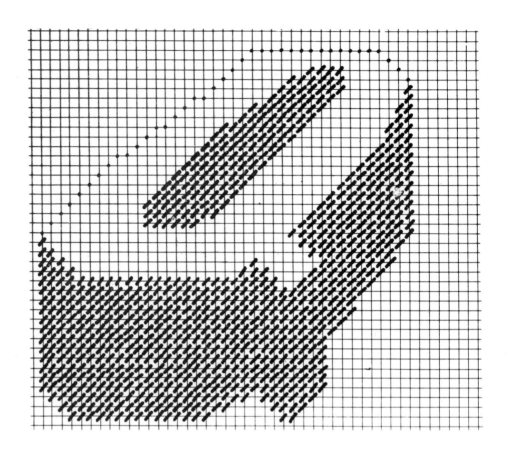

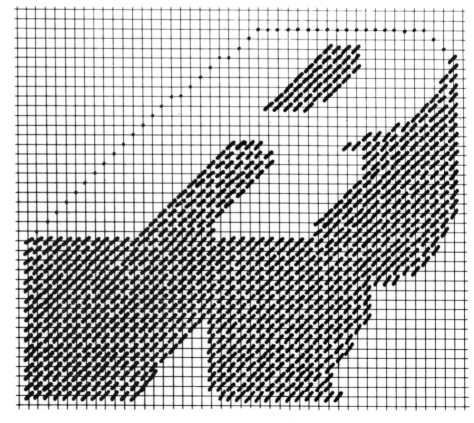

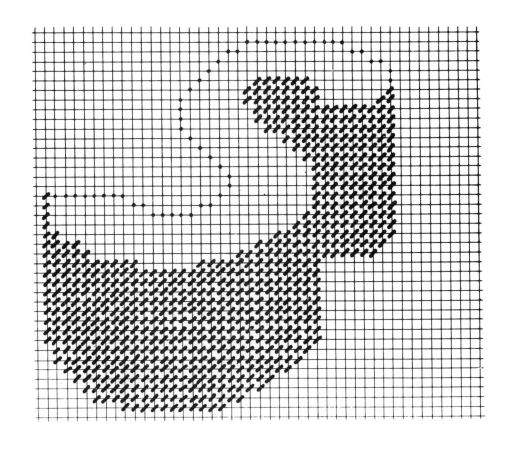

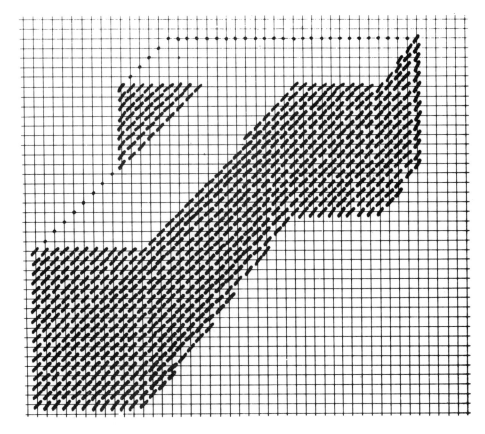

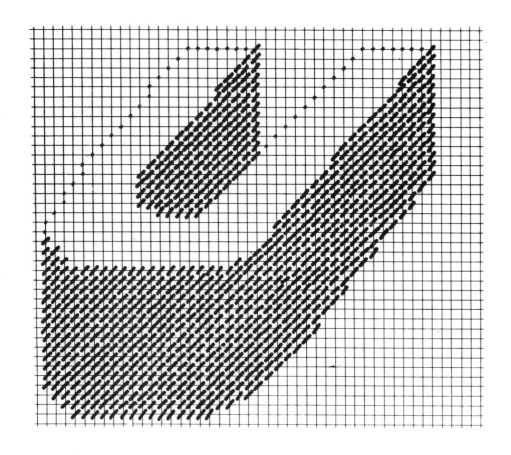

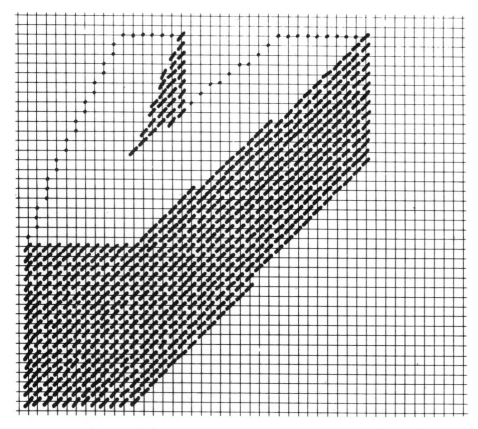

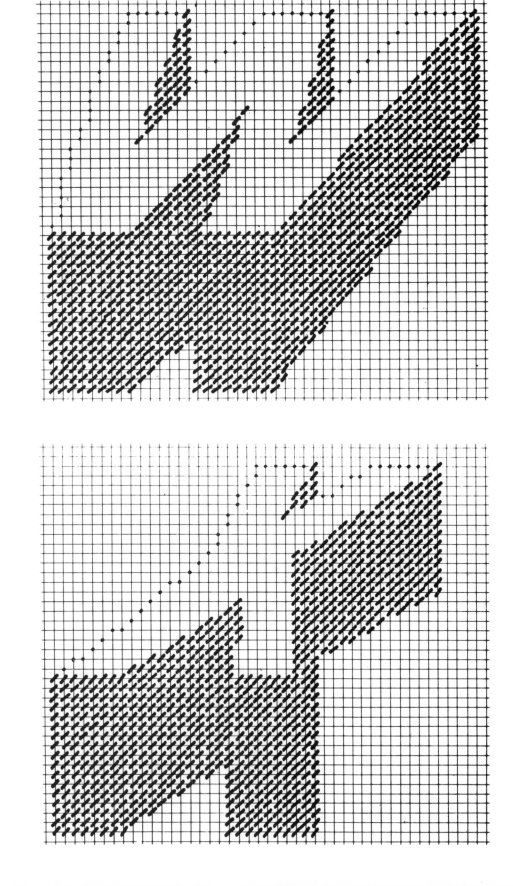

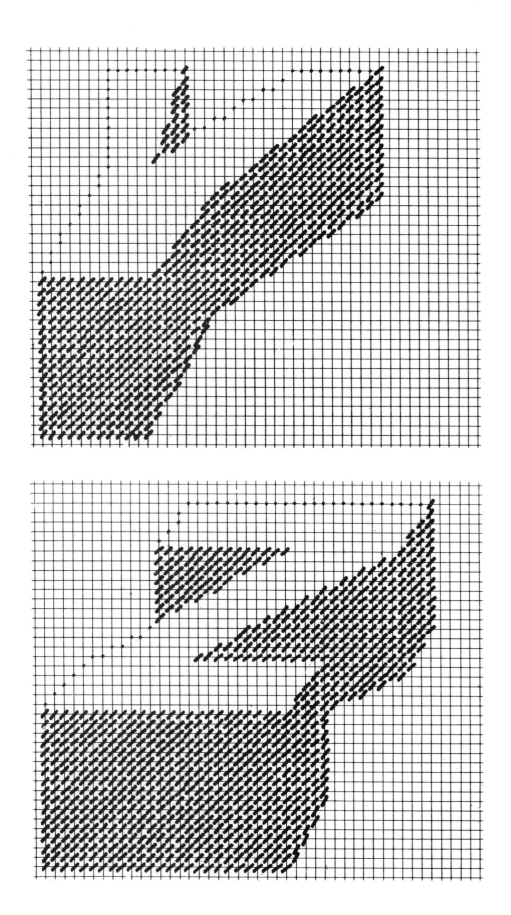

Blocking and Finishing

The instructions that follow are not detailed or complete, but rather a shorthand description for the experienced needleperson. (See the "Shopping Guide" for a recommended book of complete sewing instructions.) I feel that if you, like me, are not an expert seamstress, it might be best to entrust your labor of love to an expert.

BLOCKING

Blocking is not difficult, but achieving the best results is sometimes hard. When you have completed your needlepoint, hold it under cold water to wet it thoroughly. It need not be dripping wet, but should be moist enough to make your canvas limp. Using a heavy-duty stapler, staple your work firmly back into shape on a clean plywood board. Pull hard as you work from corner to corner. Some people use a T-square to be sure that their work is pulled back perfectly, but I generally trust my eye.

Block face-down unless you have highly textured stitches which you do not wish to flatten out.

Do not trim the edges of your work until you have blocked it. You need a good deal of raw canvas for "purchase" or pulling power, as well as for room to staple. This is why we leave at least 2 inches of unfinished canvas all around.

Regardless of the form of your finished canvas, your mesh was doubtless cut in a square or rectangular shape. Keep it that way during blocking. The original shape of your total canvas—raw as well as worked—serves as a guide to its final shape after blocking. Your actual worked canvas may be in the form of a vest, but the piece of canvas you were working on measured perhaps 24 by 18 inches. You will therefore block that piece back to 24 by 18. This will effectively pull your vest into shape as well.

Let the canvas dry overnight or longer if necessary. It should be completely dry. If needed, block several times. The Continental stitch pulls the canvas badly out of shape, and in our shop we sometimes block even small pieces three or four times. But do realize that a large piece worked in the Continental will probably never block back into its original shape because the distortion is just too great to overcome.

You may feel that a Bargello or Basketweave work need not be blocked. This is sometimes true; but in general, blocking tends to even out the stitches where the tension may have varied slightly, and it gives your work a more finished appearance.

If you are having your work framed, you may not need to block it at all, as it will get forced into shape over a stretcher or plywood backing and then nailed or stapled down permanently. If you are having your piece professionally framed, check this with your framer.

Before blocking, review "Questions and Answers: Problems and Remedies" (pages 11–15). It may save you heartache later on.

PILLOWS

Knife-edged pillows—such as the Irish Village Pillow—are the easiest to make. Cut your raw canvas to within ¾ of an inch of the worked needlepoint all around. If you plan to pipe your pillow, baste the piping in place first so the raw edge lines up with the raw canvas. The rounded pipe should be against your needlepoint, perhaps even covering the first row to ensure that no raw canvas will show through later. Join the ends of your piping in a lower corner.

Cut your backing material to allow for two ¾-inch seams. If your needlepoint pillow is 16 inches square, your fabric will measure 17½ by 17½ inches (16 inches + ¾ of an inch + ¾ of an inch). Center this face-down over your needlepoint (which should be face-up). Pin, baste, and sew along the top line of your finished work, then down the sides. Leave an opening along the bottom just large enough to insert your pillow form.

Before turning right side out, press your seams apart and back with a steam iron so they will lie as flat as possible. Cut across the four corners, removing raw mesh and fabric, close to the finished needlepoint. Starting at about 3 inches from each corner, "grade" or gradually cut the seam allowances of both fabric and raw mesh, angling toward the corners to help ensure crisp corners.

Insert a pillow form or foam rubber at least an inch larger than your pillow. If you want a fat cushion, use an even larger form. Sew your bottom opening with invisible stitches.

A box-edged pillow, such as the one copied from a fabric, is more difficult. It has been my experience that an ordinary sewing machine will not work through two layers of velvet, plus needlepoint canvas and piping. This requires a commercial machine. But a home machine may work if you are using a thinner fabric.

Your fabric backing must be the size of your pillow *plus* the size of two box edges and two ¾-inch seams. It is best to have your pillow form or foam pad on hand before starting. In this case, the form should be the same size as your finished pillow. Therefore, if your form measures 13 inches by 13 inches by 2 inches, your fabric backing will be cut 18½ inches by 18½ inches (13 inches + 2 inches + 2 inches + ¾ of an inch + ¾ of an inch). Cut carefully, and mark the exact midpoint on all four sides with straight pins. Do the same with your needlepoint. Align your needlepoint and fabric with midpoint of all sides matching face to face. Pin the two together, one side at a time, then baste and sew, always allowing for your ¾-inch seams. Once again, sew right into the first row or two of needlepoint to avoid having raw canvas show through at the turning. Leave an opening along the bottom edge large enough to insert your pillow form.

Your four corners will now stand out like large ears or ice cream cones. I believe the simplest way to get a good corner is to insert your pillow form at this point, with your work turned wrong side out. Now imagine each projecting corner as an ice cream cone, pointed at the far end and open along one side. In essence, you are going to sew closed the *mouth* of the cone from the front corner to the back corner of your pillow form, along the corner edge. Then cut away the extra fabric, leaving ¾ of an inch for seams. You will do this four times, once at each corner.

Now remove your pillow form, turn your work right side out, insert form and sew up the opening with invisible stitches.

LINING

The basic thing to remember about lining needlepoint is that whether you are working with a wallhanging, a rug, a panel, a vest, or a skirt border, the directions remain essentially the same.

For greater clarity, I will describe how to line a simple patch or pocket.

Place the lining material face-down over the needlepoint wallhanging which is face-up. Allowing a ¾-inch seam, baste and then sew all the way around, stitching through the needlepoint at least one row in from the edge. That way when the piece is turned right side out again, no raw canvas will show at the turning. Leave an opening on the bottom large enough to permit you to turn the piece right side out again. Steam press the seams back, fabric to fabric and raw canvas to needlepoint, turn the patch right side out, and stitch the opening closed with invisible stitches. If you like, steam press again, using a damp cloth on the right side of the needlepoint.

Lining a vest is really a job for a seamstress, but if you wish to try it, here is how. Line as described above with a fine matching fabric. Be sure first that both sides of the vest are exactly the same shape. If they are not, you must either add needlepoint to one, or turn back needlepoint on the other. Pin, baste, and carefully sew on the lining, leaving an opening at the bottom so you can turn your vest sides right side out. Before doing so, be sure to steam press back your fabric and raw canvas seams. Sew the opening closed with invisible stitches. Follow your vest pattern instructions for fitting and attaching the back portion of the vest. Sew frog closures on the front.

A rug or wallhanging lining is done in two sections as shown in the illustration on page 158.

FRAMING

Needlepoint can be framed in several ways. You can, if you wish, stretch the piece over a plywood board. If you decide to do this, it is best to add four flaps to the body of your finished needlepoint (one running along each side) a fraction larger than the width of the plywood being used. That is to say, if you are using ⅜-inch plywood, work flaps a fraction more than ⅜ of an inch all around. Now cut your plywood piece to the exact size of the main body of your finished needlepoint—discounting the flaps. (If your needlepoint is 18 inches by 18 inches, flaps will be 18 inches by slightly larger than ⅜ of an inch all around, and your plywood will measure just 18 inches by 18 inches by ⅜ inch.) Wrap your needlepoint around the plywood—the flaps will cover the raw wood edges—and staple down firmly in back. Cut away the extra canvas *after* you have stapled; it is helpful to have a good handhold when wrapping the canvas around the plywood.

There are some finished frames that you can buy. Lucite shadow boxes can easily accommodate needlepoint, and there are also pre-fabricated metal and wooden frames that come in stock sizes. Or buy a frame larger than needed and then mat the piece. You might wrap your needlepoint around a piece of heavy cardboard and tape it down firmly. Set it directly in the frame if it is the correct size. If your frame is larger, use matboard. Cut its outer size to fit the frame exactly, and with a razor blade or special mat knife, cut an opening—a bit smaller than your needlepoint—in the center. Set your mat in the frame, then add your needlepoint and secure it in place with masking tape.

Although I have given all these directions, it is nonetheless my strong opinion that a great frame can do wonders in setting off a beautiful work of needlepoint. And for a great frame, I believe you will need a great framer! Nevertheless, the preceding instructions will do nicely for smaller and less expensive items and gifts on which not too much time has been spent.

Shopping Guide

To obtain the items listed below, you can write directly to the manufacturer to find the retail outlet nearest you, or contact In Stitches Gallery Needlepoint, 99 Yorkville Avenue, Second Level, Toronto, Ontario, Canada.

Working from a Painted Canvas

Harper's Lady—Gemini, 720 East Jericho Turnpike, Huntington Station, New York 11746.

On the Town—K-W Designs, 17612 Beach Boulevard #17, Huntington Beach, California 92647.

Greenhouse—Sunshine Designs, 4525 Sherman Oaks Avenue, Sherman Oaks, California 91403.

Tracing Your Own Design

Floral Fabric Pillow—Schumacher Co. Inc., 919 Third Avenue, New York, New York 10022. Cotton chintz #65673, "Flower Box," 54 inches wide, 19-inch repeat. It is 100 percent cotton glaze, pigment dyed. The colorway shown is Chocolate-Bittersweet. It comes in several other colorways and has a complementary series of fabric designs labeled WLP #2357. Available through interior designers as well.

Bette Midler Record Cover—Atlantic Recording Co., 1841 Broadway, New York, New York 10023.

A Portrait—send clear black and white photo to In Stitches Gallery Needlepoint at address above for details and estimate.

Child's Director's Chairs—Gold Medal Inc., 1700 Packard Avenue, Racine, Wisconsin 53403.

Tic-Tac-Toe Doorstop—In Stitches Gallery Needlepoint, at address above.

Working from Graphs

Decorative Panel—This design is an adaptation of a Peruvian vest, translated to wallpaper by Brunschwig & Fils, collection Karjar, available through interior designers only.

Yarns

Many of the yarns listed below are carried by The Needlepoint Gallery, 151 Southeast First Ave., Boca Raton, Florida 33432.

Persian—Paternayan Bros., 312 East 95th Street, New York, New York 10029.

Silk—Kreinik Co., Parkersburg, West Virginia 26105.

Linen—Frederick Fawcett Co., 129 South Street, Boston, Massachusetts 02111.

Cotton—Joan Toggitt, 246 Fifth Avenue, New York, New York 10001.

Metallics—Elsa Williams Inc., 445 Main Street, West Townsend, Massachusetts 01474.

Velvet yarn—Idle Hands, 82-04 Lefferts Boulevard, Kew Gardens, New York 11415.

Blocking and Finishing

Helpful books in this area:

Making It With Mademoiselle. This paperback is put out by *Mademoiselle* magazine, and although not specific to needlepoint, has many helpful sewing suggestions.

Mounting Handicraft by Grete Kroncke, Van Nostrand Reinhold, 450 West 33 Street, New York, New York 10001.